The Phillies and William Penn. Back on top.

Congratulations Phillies. You proved the Curse of William Penn is officially over. And if the statue on top of the new Comcast Center had anything to do with it, we couldn't be happier. Today, you are world champions. And that's something our city can really look up to.

Comcast.

Champions!

A look back at the Phillies' triumphant 2008 season

Champions!

A LOOK BACK AT THE PHILLIES' TRIUMPHANT 2008 SEASON

By the staffs of

The Philadelphia Inquirer

PHILADELPHIA

DAILY

NEWS

THE PEOPLE PAPER

Camino Books, Inc.
Philadelphia

Champions!

DESIGN DIRECTOR
Kevin Burkett

PHOTO EDITORS
Michael Mercanti
Hai Do

CONTRIBUTING EDITORS
Josh Barnett
Pat McLoone
John Quinn
Jim Swan

WRITERS
Chuck Bausman
Bill Conlin
Paul Hagen
Bill Lyon
David Murphy
Jim Salisbury
Todd Zolecki

COPY EDITORS
Doug Darroch
Christine Sherman

PHOTO TECHNICIAN
John Gayusky

EDITORIAL ASSISTANT
Steven Sinclair Pitts

Manufactured in the United States of America

1 2 3 4 5   11 10 09 08

ISBN 978-1-933822-19-8

This book is available at a special discount on bulk purchases for promotional, business, and educational use.

Publisher
Camino Books, Inc.
P.O. Box 59026
Philadelphia, PA 19102

www.caminobooks.com

JERRY LODRIGUSS / Staff Photographer

TABLE OF CONTENTS

Foreword

BY BRIAN TIERNEY

You are holding in your hands the definitive story and photographic history of the 2008 World Series champion Philadelphia Phillies. Wow! It feels great to write that.

This book is packed with photographs and stories that document the Phillies' run to the championship. Page by thrilling page, it highlights an unbelievable season and a spirited team that may have been down but never gave up.

In heart-stopping photographs and heart-pounding accounts, "Champions!" tells the story of the National League Division Series and the National League Championship Series. It culminates with details of every thrilling moment of the 2008 World Series.

It is full of statistics, player profiles, essays and reports of a season when this Phillies team came of age and made the dream of a championship come true through determination, hard work and an unbridled will to win.

Speaking on behalf of another great home team — the local owners of The Inquirer and Daily News — I am delighted and proud to bring you this book about the Fightin' Phils. I thank our editors, reporters and photographers — the largest number of any in the region by far — who followed every minute of this team's season.

Congratulations to the 2008 World Series champions — the Philadelphia Phillies.

Brian Tierney

CEO, Philadelphia Media Holdings L.L.C.

So Taguchi, a free agent who arrived as one of baseball's premier pinch-hitters, walks to a practice field at spring training in Clearwater, Fla.

DAVID MAIALETTI / Staff Photographer

CHAPTER ONE

Lightning in a Bottle

IN A SEASON WHEN SO MUCH WENT WRONG, SOMEHOW THESE PHILS MADE IT ALL TURN OUT SO RIGHT.

BY BILL CONLIN

THE FAN APPROACHED ME at the neighborhood Wawa. He had talked Phillies baseball with me a couple of times in the past while we were checking out our breakfast sandwiches.

"I've got something in my car for you," he said. Outside, he popped his trunk and produced an empty champagne bottle, a mace that launched a thousand sips, it turned out. "I was there for the clincher. I was outside the Phillies' clubhouse when a player came out carrying this bottle. He emptied it and tossed it into a big trash can. I went to fish it out and there was another empty in there. So I scored them both. Great souvenir, huh? I'd like you to have one."

I thanked him and took it home. The fireplace was on in the den, paying homage to the early cold snap — I hope the parade doesn't get snowed out. As a kid, I liked to take my emerald green, 6.5-ounce Coke bottle and stare at the fire through the bottom and watch the flames play tricks through the glass.

I held the champagne bottle to my right eye and stared at the fire through that little dimple they put on the bottom for some reason.

A voice filled the den.

"Well, expert, have you figured out how this team managed to win 11 postseason games?"

"It wasn't easy," I stammered.

"I'm going to run the season by you on a slow reel, leading with all the reasons why they shouldn't have won. Just blink to change the time frame."

"Fire away."

Suddenly, it was last November. Brad Lidge, the new closer, was meeting the media after his trade from Houston. There was something wrong with that picture. Brad came into the press conference room on crutches. Not good, although we were promised he would be OK by spring training.

Jimmy Rollins, converging here with Pedro Feliz on a pop fly, missed most of April and part of May with an ankle injury.

I blinked. The scene shifted to Phils at Mets in the eighth game of the season. It is the eighth inning and Jimmy Rollins, the 2007 MVP, appeared to jam an ankle sliding back into second base. He scored a run, but Eric Bruntlett went to shortstop in the Mets' half. The man who played all 162 games last season would not be in the lineup for the next 27.

Blink. Blink. Jimmy just failed to run hard on a fly he popped to no-man's land in shallow left. The ball is dropped, but Rollins jogged to first and was unable to take second on the misplay. Manager Charlie Manuel, who loves his normally feisty shortstop like a son, waited until the end of the inning and sent Bruntlett out to play short. It was an instant cause celebre.

That scene dissolved and now Rollins was behind the wheel of a very expensive auto, stuck in gridlocked, late-morning, mid-Manhattan traffic. Manuel has two rules. Hustle. Be on time. J-Roll arrived at Shea Stadium unfashionably late. The manager played Bruntlett at short. The Phils' top-of-the-lineup catalyst had violated both of Manuel's rules in half a season. Jimmy compounded the felony by insisting

Charlie overreacted and was wrong this time.

Blink. The scene rewound to the first formal workout of spring training. Lidge was on a practice mound. Cameras were whirring as he coiled and delivered his first warmup pitch. A cleat caught as he turned on the rubber and something went click in his mending right knee. Potential headline: "Bury Phils season at Wounded Knee."

Rollins hurt, then yanked for loafing, then benched for lateness ... Lidge on crutches, then reinjured and missing the entire exhibition season ... Manuel cheerfully saying, "Tom Gordon can pitch two to three days in a row as long as he doesn't throw more than about 20 pitches in any game."

In another flicker of flame and imagination, it was Opening Day and Brett Myers was OK, serviceable but hardly the ace the Phillies hoped would justify his controversial switch from closer back to the rotation to make room for Lidge. And everybody knew that putting the emotional Myers ahead of Cole Hamels in the pecking order was merely a band-aid for his fragile psyche.

Blink. It was a warm night in a crowded ballpark

Brad Lidge, who had knee surgery after the 2007 season, receives attention after reinjuring it on his first pitch in spring training. He wasn't ready for Opening Day, but went on to go 41-for-41 in save opportunities.

DAVID M WARREN / Staff Photographer

Phillies Opening Day starter Brett Myers joined the Triple A Lehigh Valley IronPigs in July but returned to the majors as one of the best pitchers in the National League.

in Allentown and Brett Myers was making the first of four minor league starts. The righthander had agreed to be optioned after a series of horrific outings that left his ERA on life support and Manuel's rotation in disarray. But it was really a rehab assignment to rescue his skewed delivery and patch his confidence back together.

Brett's final start was for the Class A Clearwater Threshers. Now it was the first inning of his return to the Phillies, July 23. And he had just walked his fourth consecutive Met to force in a run. His next start would be against the Nationals. Myers is brilliant this time, allowing an unearned run and four hits in seven innings. The scene faded with Lidge being congratulated for his 25th save. Only perfect and on his way to 41 saves without blowing one.

Blink. I shifted the champagne bottle to my left hand for a visit to the engine room and MVP candidates Chase Utley and Ryan Howard. It was Aug. 13 in Dodger Stadium. The Phillies were three losses into a four-game sweep by a team struggling with .500, the same team they would take out 4-1 in the NLCS. Utley's power numbers were down amid conjecture he was playing with a tear in a hip labrum,

a left-wrist injury, or both. Baseball's best second baseman was hitless in a 7-6 loss. But Howard blasted his 33rd homer of an absolutely bizarre season. In a season where he tied his former strikeout record of 199 and committed more errors, 19, than any Phillies first baseman in more than a half-century, Howard performed a very deep knee bend, lifted his team onto his back and carried it through September. Ryan finished with either the worst great season in slugging history or the greatest lousy season.

I blinked my way through another uneven but gritty and productive season by Pat Burrell, brief hot streaks lapsing into long droughts. But the droughts always seemed to be broken by a home run or huge hit that ignited a rally or sealed a victory.

When Jamie Moyer flickered onto the bottom of the champagne bottle, the color changed from emerald to the sepia tone of the pre-Technicolor opening of "The Wizard of Oz." He was in a rocking chair, Auntie Em, throwing pitch after pitch just off the plate or jamming righthanded sluggers with cut fastballs on their hands.

I caught Kyle Kendrick returning to earth, but it was a soft landing because GM Pat Gillick's trade-

Ryan Howard, who tied his old record of 199 strikeouts, led the major leagues in homers with 48 and RBI with 146.

RON CORTES / Staff Photographer

Fans cheer Kyle Kendrick, a surprise contributor to the 2007 NL East champions, who went 11-9 in 2008 but later fell on hard times.

week pickup, Joe Blanton, kept the Phillies in most of his starts. And rookie J.A. Happ pitched with poise and skill whenever he was handed the ball.

The only trouble with brilliant Cole Hamels was that whenever he pitched, he appeared to transfix two offenses — the opponent's and his own. Lack of run support might have cost him a 20-victory season.

The champagne bottle was at my feet when I blinked awake. I was on my own to make rhyme and reason of how a team that shot itself in the foot so often was able to sidestep so many potential disasters and win the 11 games now required to become World Series champion.

One answer is an easy one: good health. The rotation stayed remarkably intact. Even Adam Eaton, dreadful most of the time, didn't break down. If Rollins had been out much more than a month, it could have been devastating. And after his walkabouts — I think his ankle restricted him more than he let on — Rollins stopped trying to make up the stats from the lost month and was content to merely be one of the game's premier shortstops.

Shane Victorino infuriated the usually unflappable Manuel with a few bursts of bonehead baseball. But at the end of the season, the Flyin' Hawaiian was the team's most exciting and explosive player on both sides of the ball. Angular and deceptively fast and powerful Jayson Werth told the manager he thought he could play every day. Manuel replied that all he had to do was hit righthanders a little better. Werth obliged.

But I probably answered my own question best a few paragraphs back by using the word "team."

The seven-month baseball season puts a premium on roster chemistry. It tests character and endurance. Charlie Manuel has proved beyond refuting that he is the perfect manager, mentor and father figure for a roster where Pat Gillick, a master roster builder, did perhaps the best patching-and-filling job of his great career.

Sure Pat Gillick made mistakes. Many of them. But in a game where batters who fail two-thirds of the time are locks for Hall of Fame election, is it fair to expect a general manager to be perfect?

The champagne bottle from that raucous clubhouse celebration will go on the fireplace mantle right under the panoramic photo of the final game in Veterans Stadium. It represents 25 years of pent-up frustration. I wonder if it can look ahead to 2009? ●

Shane Victorino, whose grand slam sparked the Phillies' win in Game 2 of the NLDS, is followed in the postgame high-five line by Jayson Werth, Eric Bruntlett, Jimmy Rollins and Chase Utley.

STEVEN M. FALK / Staff Photographer

Charlie Manuel, a father figure who doled out tough love when it was needed, proved to be the right manager at the right time for this team.

YONG KIM / Staff Photographer

Postseason Roster

Joe Blanton 56

Position: Pitcher

H/W: 6-3, 255

Born: Dec. 11, 1980, in Nashville, Tenn.

Bats: Right

Throws: Right

How we got him: Trade with A's in July for prospects Adrian Cardenas, Josh Outman and Matt Spencer.

Eric Bruntlett 4

Position: Utility

H/W: 6-0, 190

Born: March 29, 1978, in Lafayette, Ind.

Bats: Right

Throws: Right

How we got him: Trade with Astros in November 2007 (with Brad Lidge) for Michael Bourn, Mike Costanzo and Geoff Geary.

Pat Burrell 5

Position: Outfielder

H/W: 6-4, 234

Born: Oct. 10, 1976, in Eureka Springs, Ark.

Bats: Right

Throws: Right

How we got him: Taken by Phillies in the first round of the 1998 draft (first pick overall).

Clay Condrey 55

Position: Pitcher

H/W: 6-3, 215

Born: Nov. 19, 1975 in Beaumont, Texas

Bats: Right

Throws: Right

How we got him: Trade with Padres in March 2004 for Trino Aguilar.

Chris Coste 27

Position: Catcher

H/W: 6-1, 215

Born: Feb. 4, 1973, in Fargo, N.D.

Bats: Right

Throws: Right

How we got him: Signed as minor league free agent in October 2004.

Greg Dobbs 19

Position: Utility

H/W: 6-1, 205

Born: July 2, 1978, in Los Angeles

Bats: Left

Throws: Right

How we got him: Claimed off waivers from Mariners in January 2007.

Chad Durbin 37

Position: Pitcher

H/W: 6-2, 200

Born: Dec. 3, 1977, in Spring Valley, Ill.

Bats: Right

Throws: Right

How we got him: Signed as a free agent in December 2007.

Scott Eyre 47

Position: Pitcher

H/W: 6-1, 220

Born: May 30, 1972, in Inglewood, Calif.

Bats: Left

Throws: Left

How we got him: Trade with Cubs for minor league righthander Brian Schlitter.

Pedro Feliz 7

Position: Third base

H/W: 6-1, 180

Born: April 27, 1975, in Azua, Dom. Rep.

Bats: Right

Throws: Right

How we got him: Signed as a free agent in January 2008.

Cole Hamels 35

Position: Pitcher

H/W: 6-3, 190

Born: Dec. 27, 1983, in San Diego

Bats: Left

Throws: Left

How we got him: Taken by Phillies in the first round of the 2002 draft (17th pick overall).

Postseason Roster (continued)

J.A. Happ 43

Position: Pitcher
H/W: 6-6, 200
Born: Oct. 19, 1982, in Spring Valley, Ill.
Bats: Left
Throws: Left
How we got him: Taken by Phillies in the third round of the 2003 draft.

Ryan Howard 6

Position: First base
H/W: 6-4, 230
Born: Nov. 19, 1979, in St. Louis
Bats: Left
Throws: Left
How we got him: Taken by Phillies in the fifth round of the 2001 draft.

Geoff Jenkins 10

Position: Outfielder
H/W: 6-1, 215
Born: July 21, 1974, in Olympia, Wash.
Bats: Left
Throws: Right
How we got him: Signed as a free agent in December 2007.

Brad Lidge 54

Position: Pitcher
H/W: 6-5, 210
Born: Dec. 23, 1976, in Sacramento, Calif.
Bats: Right
Throws: Right
How we got him: Trade with Astros in November 2007 (with Eric Bruntlett) for Michael Bourn, Mike Costanzo and Geoff Geary.

Ryan Madson 63

Position: Pitcher
H/W: 6-6, 200
Born: Aug. 28, 1980, in Long Beach, Calif.
Bats: Left
Throws: Right
How we got him: Taken by Phillies in the ninth round of the 1998 draft.

Jamie Moyer 50

Position: Pitcher
H/W: 6-0, 185
Born: Nov. 18, 1962, in Sellersville, Pa.
Bats: Left
Throws: Left
How we got him: Trade with Mariners in August 2006 for pitchers Andrew Baldwin and Andrew Barb.

Brett Myers 39

Position: Pitcher
H/W: 6-4, 240
Born: Aug. 17, 1980, in Jacksonville, Fla.
Bats: Right
Throws: Right
How we got him: Taken by Phillies in the first round of the 1999 draft (12th overall).

Jimmy Rollins 11

Position: Shortstop
H/W: 5-8, 160
Born: Nov. 27, 1978, in Oakland, Calif.
Bats: Both
Throws: Right
How we got him: Taken by Phillies in the second round of the 1996 draft.

J.C. Romero 16

Position: Pitcher
H/W: 5-11, 203
Born: June 4, 1976, in Rio Pedras, P.R.
Bats: Both
Throws: Left
How we got him: Signed as free agent in June 2007.

Carlos Ruiz 51

Position: Catcher
H/W: 6-0, 170
Born: Jan. 22, 1979, in David, Panama
Bats: Right
Throws: Right
How we got him: Signed as an amateur free agent in December 1998.

Postseason Roster (continued)

Matt Stairs 12

Position: Outfielder

H/W: 5-9, 210

Born: Feb. 27, 1968, in St. John, New Brunswick, Canada

Bats: Left

Throws: Right

How we got him: Trade with Blue Jays for Fabio Castro in August.

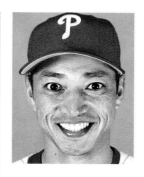

So Taguchi 99

Position: Outfielder

H/W: 5-10, 163

Born: July 2, 1969, in Hyogo Prefecture, Japan

Bats: Right

Throws: Right

How we got him: Signed as a free agent in December 2007.

Chase Utley 26

Position: Second base

H/W: 6-1, 200

Born: Dec. 17, 1978, in Pasadena, Calif.

Bats: Left

Throws: Right

How we got him: Taken by Phillies in the first round of the 2000 draft (15th overall).

Shane Victorino 8

Position: Outfielder

H/W: 5-9, 180

Born: Nov. 30, 1980, in Wailuku, Hawaii

Bats: Both

Throws: Right

How we got him: Selected from the Dodgers in December 2004 in the Rule 5 draft.

Jayson Werth 28

Position: Outfielder

H/W: 6-5, 190

Born: May 20, 1979, in Springfield, Ill.

Bats: Right

Throws: Right

How we got him: Signed as a free agent in December 2006.

THE REST OF THE 40-MAN ROSTER

No.	Name	Position	H	W	Bat/Throw	Born	Hometown	'08 Games
49	Joe Bisenius	Pitcher	6-4	205	R/R	Sept. 18, 1982	Sioux City, Iowa	0
46	Andrew Carpenter	Pitcher	6-3	225	R/R	May 18, 1985	Grants Pass, Ore.	1
21	Adam Eaton	Pitcher	6-2	200	R/R	Nov. 23, 1977	Seattle	21
45	Tom Gordon*	Pitcher	5-10	200	R/R	Nov. 18, 1967	Sebring, Fla.	34
38	Kyle Kendrick	Pitcher	6-3	190	R/R	Aug. 26, 1984	Houston	31
47	Scott Mathieson*	Pitcher	6-3	190	R/R	Feb. 27, 1984	Vancouver, Canada	0
—	Scott Nestor	Pitcher	6-4	225	R/R	Aug. 20, 1984	La Canada, Calif.	0
57	Rudy Seanez	Pitcher	6-1	225	R/R	Oct. 20, 1968	Brawley, Calif.	42
44	Les Walrond	Pitcher	6-3	205	L/L	Nov. 7, 1976	Muskogee, Okla.	6
59	Michael Zagurski*	Pitcher	6-0	225	L/L	Jan. 27, 1983	Omaha, Neb.	0
23	Jason Jaramillo	Catcher	6-0	200	S/R	Oct. 9, 1982	Racine, Wisc.	0
3	Lou Marson	Catcher	6-1	200	R/R	June 26, 1986	Scottsdale, Ariz.	1
24	Mike Cervenak	Infielder	5-11	195	R/R	Aug. 17, 1976	Trenton, Mich.	10
18	Brad Harman	Infielder	6-1	195	R/R	Nov. 19, 1985	Melbourne, Australia	6
9	Tadahito Iguchi	Infielder	5-10	185	R/R	Dec. 4, 1974	Tokyo, Japan	85
33	Andy Tracy	Infielder	6-3	220	L/R	Dec. 11, 1973	Bowling Green, Ohio	4
40	Greg Golson	Outfielder	6-0	190	R/R	Sept. 17, 1985	Austin, Texas	6

* On 60-day disabled list

CHAPTER TWO

The Curse, Reversed

FOR THE FIRST TIME SINCE
THE CITY ROSE ABOVE BILLY PENN,
WE HAVE A WINNER IN TOWN.

BY BILL LYON

I T'S A LONG, LONG ROAD that has no turning.

And so, at long, long last, for the impassioned, long-suffering, victory-famished fans of Philadelphia, some day has finally arrived.

The Phillies have won the World Series. Cue the choir. Hallelujah ... Hallelujah ... and Amen.

No more curse. No more hex. No more jinx. No more devil medicine. No more witch doctors with pins and dolls. No more mumbo-mojo. No more of that voodoo that you do so well.

No, the shroud of suffocating defeat and despair that has hung over us for a quarter of a century has been lifted. The funeral dirge is replaced by a joyous, whooping, trumpets-blaring, cymbals-crashing parade.

The major league baseball team of Philadelphia has delivered unto us our first champion since the 76ers in 1983. No fans in other cities with four professional teams have wandered, lost and lonely and unfulfilled, for so long. Ah, but what we do best, what even foes must grudgingly admit, is suffer

Inquirer archives

The William Penn statue atop City Hall was dwarfed when One Liberty Place rose to become the city's tallest structure in 1987.

The fans cheer during Game 1 of the NLCS (left) — ever mindful that the Phillies had gone without a World Series title since 1980.

STEVEN M. FALK / Staff Photographer

grandly. We keep coming back for more, despite all the losing. Now, our persistence is rewarded.

It seems only fitting that it is the Fightins who have quenched our thirst for they have suffered the ignominy of losing more games than any team in any sport ... ever. During the summer of 2007, they succumbed for the 10,000th time.

Now, all is forgiven. Well, almost all. This is Philly, after all.

It is not as though World Series championships come around here on a regular basis.

This is No. 2.

In 126 years.

Ah, but the waiting makes the champagne all the sweeter.

This team has achieved what the others, the ones wearing cleats or sneaks or skates, could not. Always before, when one of our band of mercenaries stood on the threshold of triumph, rather than stride boldly across it, they would trip and collapse in an unsightly heap.

Seven times since 1983 one of our four teams has played for the championship, and seven times calamity has visited them. A walkoff home run here, an interception there, and ... well, the litany of frustration is a familiar one, known to all, by heart, retold around the campfires.

But here come the new Fightins, a likable, blithespirited bunch with names that sound like the roll call for the cast of a soap opera: Chase and Cole. Ryan and Shane. Brad and Brett. Jimmy and Jayson.

With them the future, for a change, brims with promise. For the core of this title team is homegrown and young, and it is unsaddled by the crushing weight of past failures. When asked about The Curse, they shrug and wave it away. It does not belong to them.

Cole Hamels, the pitching prodigy, is 24. He was yet to be born when the famine set in. Asked to describe this team, he said: "We are lighthearted."

Not exactly the sort of response you would expect from the vast majority of athletes, but revealing nonetheless. For Hamels and the rest of the Fightins, the draping of clothes around the statue of Billy Penn, a wardrobe act that many zealots believe is responsible for the famine, is only so much talk. And ancient

Phillies' All-Time Regular-Season Records

The Phillies have recorded **8,945 wins and 10,098 losses** since their debut in 1883 (an all-time .470 winning percentage). Their record this year was one game better than in 1980, when they won their only other World Series.

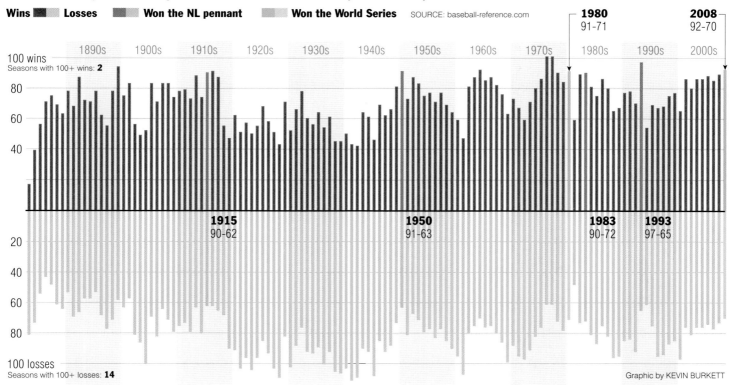

Graphic by KEVIN BURKETT

Blame Game

Since the Sixers won the NBA championship in 1983, Philadelphia had experienced the longest championship drought in history among four-team cities — until this year.

1983: The **Phillies** lose the World Series to the Baltimore Orioles in five games.

1985: The **Flyers** lose the Stanley Cup finals to the Edmonton Oilers in five games.

1987: One Liberty Place surpasses City Hall as the city's tallest building. Two months later …

… The **Flyers** lose the Stanley Cup finals for the second time in three years to the Edmonton Oilers, in seven games.

 **1993:** The **Phillies** lose the World Series to the Toronto Blue Jays in six games.

« 1997: The **Flyers** lose the Stanley Cup finals to the Detroit Red Wings in four games.

2001: The **Sixers** lose the NBA Finals to the Los Angeles Lakers in five games.

2005: The **Eagles**, after losing the NFC title game in their three previous seasons, lose Super Bowl XXXIX to the New England Patriots, 24-21, in February 2005.

— Kevin Burkett

history. Same for those who think the erection of buildings taller than Penn's hat is a blatant act of spitting into the wind.

This triumph may scrub away the bittersweet fatalism that has dogged us for so long. Negadelphia, that self-fulfilling expect-the-worst civic philosophy, may at last be put to rest.

Hard to play here, we are told by those who do, when so many expect the losing to continue.

As Jimmy Rollins, the shortstop and 2007 Most Valuable Player, put it: "Everyone should just remember that nothing comes easy in Philadelphia."

No, it doesn't. But if it did, perhaps this would not feel so exhilarating.

In the pages that follow, you will relive the Phillies' magic carpet ride.

It is not the destination that matters, we are endlessly reminded, rather it is the journey itself.

But you know what is best of all? To have the best of both. ●

SARAH J. GLOVER / Staff Photographer

In an attempt to reverse the curse, this two-foot-tall miniature of the William Penn statue was attached to a girder and placed at the top of the Comcast Center, now Philadelphia's tallest building.

2007 MVP Jimmy Rollins said that "Everyone should just remember that nothing comes easy in Philadelphia." He is being congratulated here by Scott Eyre after the team won the NLCS.

Jimmy Rollins waits to bat
on a misty Opening Day.
The Nats won the game, 11-6.

YONG KIM / Staff Photographer

CHAPTER THREE
The Regular Season

PHILS' DEPTH AND GRIT
SAVE A SEASON THREATENED
BY INJURIES AND SLUMPS.

BY DAVID MURPHY

AN UGLY BLANKET OF CLOUDS hung over Citizens Bank Park as Brett Myers and the rest of the Philadelphia Phillies arrived for their season-opening game against the Washington Nationals. A light mist fell on the tarp that covered the field. Everyone from players to groundskeepers to the media eyed the skies with a certain wariness.

Another Opening Day, another season. And what a great way to start.

The weather eventually cooperated, but the outlook didn't get much sunnier on the field. With newly acquired Phillies closer Brad Lidge still on the mend from knee surgery, a Washington team pegged to finish last in the National League East exploded for five runs in the top of the ninth inning to crack open a tied game and send the Phillies to their third straight season-opening loss.

Nationals 11, Phillies 6.

But the lasting memory of the game was not the notch in the loss column, nor the struggles of the pitching staff, nor the feeling that the potent Phillies offense had left runs on the field.

No, the lasting memory of Opening Day 2008 was the lack of panic emanating from the locker stalls that line the walls of the oval home clubhouse. There were shoulder shrugs, and a few eye rolls, and that time-honored athletic cliche.

One day at a time.

"I'm going to say it over and over again," second baseman Chase Utley said, "but that's the mentality you have to take."

Over the next 161 games, spanning six months of the calendar year, that mentality served these Phil-

Jimmy Rollins, who had said the Phillies were capable of a 100-win season, tosses his bat after homering in the Opening Day loss.

YONG KIM / Staff Photographer

lies well. They entered the season riding the wave of goodwill that accompanied their dramatic 2007 stretch run, when they overcame a seven-game deficit with 17 to play to win their first division title since the fabled 1993 season. Shortstop Jimmy Rollins, who made headlines the previous offseason when he labeled the Phillies the team to beat in the NL East, casually floated the idea that the 2008 Phils were capable of winning 100 games. Despite having to contend against a New York Mets team that had added ace lefthander Johan Santana in the offseason, there was an air of confidence about the squad.

That confidence never evaporated.

Less than two weeks after that Opening Day loss to the Nationals, the Phillies were dealt what appeared at the time to be a crippling blow. In the eighth inning of a 5-2 win over the Mets, Rollins slid into second base on a fake pickoff attempt and came up lame. He finished the game and spent the next few days downplaying the injury. But after a week-and-a-half without the 2007 MVP in the lineup, the Phillies placed him on the disabled list with a sprained left ankle. He wound up missing a month.

A few days later, starting centerfielder Shane Victorino suffered a strained calf in a game against the Cubs and was immediately placed on the disabled list. For nearly two weeks, the Phillies played without their No. 1 and No. 2 hitters in the lineup. On April 13, the day after Victorino went down, manager Charlie Manuel batted rightfielder Geoff Jenkins leadoff. The next game, Jayson Werth and Carlos Ruiz — the No. 7 and No. 8 hitters on Opening Day — batted No. 1 and No. 2.

The Phillies lost four of their first six games without Victorino and Rollins. Two of those losses came in a home series against the Mets. After that series, as they prepared to embark on a seven-game road trip, the Phillies were 9-10 and in fourth place in the division. Twelve-hundred miles to the south, a new contender was emerging in Miami, where the Florida Marlins were 11-7 and in first place.

"If you stop and think about it, one guy can hurt your whole season," Manuel said at the time, referring to the injuries. "This is a game where you can't afford to lose too many games."

But the Phillies passed their early test. They won five of their first six games on the road trip, sweeping a two-game series against the Colorado Rockies, splitting two with the Milwaukee Brewers, then taking two of three from the Pirates in Pittsburgh. By

Regular Season by the Numbers

INDIVIDUAL HITTING STATS

Name	AB	R	H	2B	3B	HR	RBI	BB	BA
Joe Blanton	16	0	1	0	0	0	1	0	.063
Eric Bruntlett	212	37	46	9	1	2	15	21	.217
Pat Burrell	536	74	134	33	3	33	86	102	.250
Mike Cervenak	13	0	2	0	0	0	1	0	.154
Chris Coste	274	28	72	17	0	9	36	16	.263
Greg Dobbs	226	30	68	14	1	9	40	11	.301
Chad Durbin	9	0	1	0	0	0	0	0	.111
Adam Eaton	28	1	5	2	0	0	1	5	.179
Pedro Feliz	425	43	106	19	2	14	58	33	.249
Cole Hamels	76	3	17	2	0	0	3	0	.224
J.A. Happ	7	0	0	0	0	0	0	0	.000
Brad Harman	10	1	1	1	0	0	1	1	.100
Ryan Howard	610	105	153	26	4	48	146	81	.251
Tadahito Iguchi	310	29	72	15	1	2	24	26	.232
Geoff Jenkins	293	27	72	16	0	9	29	24	.246
Kyle Kendrick	50	3	5	1	0	0	2	3	.100
Jamie Moyer	51	4	4	1	0	0	1	7	.078
Brett Myers	58	3	4	1	0	0	1	4	.069
Jimmy Rollins	556	76	154	38	9	11	59	58	.277
Carlos Ruiz	320	47	70	14	0	4	31	44	.219
Matt Stairs	17	4	5	1	0	2	5	1	.294
So Taguchi	91	18	20	5	1	0	9	8	.220
Chase Utley	607	113	177	41	4	33	104	64	.292
Shane Victorino	570	102	167	30	8	14	58	45	.293
Jayson Werth	418	73	114	16	3	24	67	57	.273
Team totals	**5,509**	**799**	**1,407**	**291**	**36**	**214**	**762**	**586**	**.255**

INDIVIDUAL PITCHING STATS

Name	W-L	ERA	G	SV	R	ER	H	BB	SO
Joe Blanton	4-0	4.20	13	0	36	33	66	31	49
Andrew Carpenter	0-0	0.00	1	0	0	0	1	1	1
Clay Condrey	3-4	3.26	56	1	26	25	85	19	34
Chad Durbin	5-4	2.87	71	1	33	28	81	35	63
Adam Eaton	4-8	5.80	21	0	71	69	131	44	57
Scott Eyre	5-0	4.21	38	0	12	12	23	7	32
Tom Gordon	5-4	5.16	34	2	19	17	31	17	26
Cole Hamels	14-10	3.09	33	0	89	78	193	53	196
J.A. Happ	1-0	3.69	8	0	13	13	28	14	26
Kyle Kendrick	11-9	5.49	31	0	103	95	194	57	68
Brad Lidge	2-0	1.95	72	41	17	15	50	35	92
Ryan Madson	4-2	3.05	76	1	29	28	79	23	67
Jamie Moyer	16-7	3.71	33	0	85	81	199	62	123
Brett Myers	10-13	4.55	30	0	103	96	197	65	163
J.C. Romero	4-4	2.75	81	1	18	18	41	38	52
Rudy Seanez	5-4	3.53	42	0	24	17	38	25	30
R.J. Swindle	0-0	7.71	3	0	4	4	9	2	4
Les Walrond	1-1	6.10	6	0	7	7	13	9	12
Team totals	**92-70**	**3.88**	**162**	**47**	**680**	**625**	**1,444**	**533**	**1,081**

Pat Burrell receives a hero's welcome after his two-run homer in the 10th inning beat San Francisco, 6-5, on May 2. Ex-Phillie Aaron Rowand had homered for the Giants in the top half of the inning.

STEVEN M. FALK / Staff Photographer

Phillies fans express themselves at the regular-season finale. For the previous 15 years, it was all bust, no World Series.

the time Victorino returned to the lineup on May 1, the Phillies were 16-13 and in first place. The heroes of the first month were Utley and Pat Burrell, who took turns slugging their way to victory. Of the 133 runs the Phillies had scored through April, Utley and Burrell had combined to drive in 48. Utley finished the month with 11 home runs and a .360 batting average. Burrell was hitting .326 with eight home runs and a .452 on-base percentage.

Nobody knew it at the time, but a precedent had been set. For all the preseason talk of the collective potential of the Phillies' lineup — Manuel was asked on several occasions by reporters if he thought his team might finish the season with more than 1,000 runs — the difference between winning and losing would often come down to the stellar efforts of one or two of its members.

As the season wore on, the production by Utley and Burrell leveled out. Both players found themselves in slumps. But in their place rose a new crop of stars.

At the plate, players like Victorino and Werth made the transition from role players to budding stars. One of the highlights of the season came on May 16 at Citizens Bank Park against the Toronto Blue Jays. Werth, who began the season sharing time with Jen-

kins in rightfield, hit home runs in his first three at-bats to tie a Phillies record. In the 10-3 victory over the Blue Jays, Werth drove in all but two runs.

Eleven years after the Orioles drafted him as a high school catcher, the 29-year-old outfielder basked in what to that point was the best game of his life. Werth's career, a microcosm of the Phillies' season, had nearly been ended in 2005 while he was with the Dodgers when a spring-training pitch hit him on the left wrist. The injury hampered him throughout what was supposed to be a breakout season. After undergoing surgery, he missed all of 2006. The Phillies signed him before the 2007 season. Although he played a pivotal role in the Phillies' stretch run that year, he entered this season viewed only as a platoon player in rightfield. On that May night, things began to change.

By the end of the year — aided in part by a quad strain suffered by Jenkins in late August — Werth was the team's everyday rightfielder, setting career highs with 24 home runs and 67 RBI while hitting .273.

"It's tough to get opportunities in this game," Werth said back in May. "That's one thing that they give out very rarely is everyday opportunities. I had a chance in LA, then I got hurt, and I was able to get healthy

Young fans learn it's a lot easier catching a ball when there aren't other hands and gloves reaching for it.

and come here. It was a blessing in disguise, I guess."

The ability to fight through adversity was a hallmark of the 2008 Phillies. There was Victorino, who was written off by the Los Angeles Dodgers and San Diego Padres before landing in Philadelphia. In his first season as an everyday centerfielder, the 5-9 Hawaiian hit .293 with 14 home runs, 58 RBI and 36 stolen bases. On June 6 in Atlanta, Victorino drove in the go-ahead run with a 10th-inning triple, then threw out the tying run at the plate to preserve the 4-3 victory. On Aug. 3, Victorino's three-run homer in the top of the eighth inning was the big blow in the Phillies' 5-4 comeback win in St. Louis.

Midway through September, the Phillies found themselves in their most precarious position of the season. After dropping the final two games of a series against the Marlins, they trailed the Mets by 3½ games in the NL East. Furthermore, they were four games behind the Brewers in the wild-card standings.

But with 16 games to play and their playoff hopes reduced to a glimmer, the Phillies once again battled back. They swept the Brewers in a four-game series at Citizens Bank Park, highlighted by a dominant effort by a rejuvenated Myers in the nightcap of a Sunday doubleheader. Myers, who had an abysmal first half and spent three weeks in the minor leagues before the All-Star break, pitched a two-hitter as the Phillies beat Milwaukee, 6-1.

The season turned. Tied for the wild-card lead and a game behind the Mets in the division, the Phillies won nine of their final 12 games. Ryan Howard, who struggled throughout the early part of the season, hit .352 with 11 home runs and 32 RBI in September. The Phillies beat the Nationals, 4-3, on Sept. 27 to secure their second straight division title.

Jamie Moyer, the 45-year-old lefthander, recorded the win that day. Lidge, acquired in a trade with the Astros, recorded the save to finish a perfect 41-for-41 on the season. Lefthander Cole Hamels, who went 14-10 with a 3.09 ERA, skipped his scheduled start in the meaningless regular-season finale to rest for the playoffs.

As the Phillies celebrated the division title on the field after the game, a light mist of rain mixed with the spray of champagne. Looking back to Opening Day, it seemed appropriate. ●

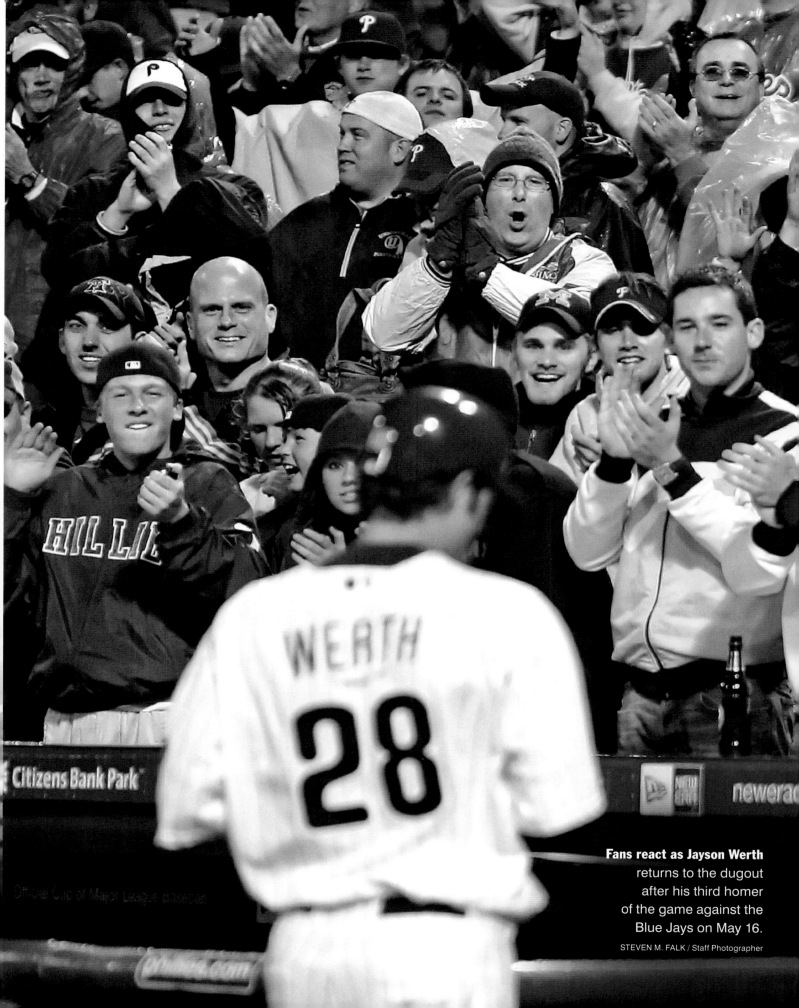

Fans react as Jayson Werth returns to the dugout after his third homer of the game against the Blue Jays on May 16.

STEVEN M. FALK / Staff Photographer

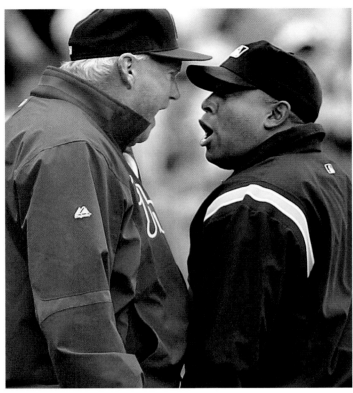

DAVID MAIALETTI / Staff Photographer

Charlie Manuel earns a heave-ho from third-base ump Adrian Johnson, who ruled Mark DeRosa's foul ball a home run in the Phillies' 6-5, 10-inning loss to the Cubs on April 13.

RON CORTES / Staff Photographer

Jimmy Rollins is safe at first as Nationals first baseman Nick Johnson is pulled off the bag.

Chase Utley, whose hot start sparked MVP speculation, homers to right in the season opener.

JERRY LODRIGUSS / Staff Photographer

Chase Utley greets So Taguchi, who scored the winning run in the 12th inning against the Diamondbacks on July 11, on a hit by Jayson Werth.

Cole Hamels went 14-10, but his 3.09 ERA suggests he could have won 20 games.

Shane Victorino gets what he deserves after singling in the winning run against the Mets in the ninth inning on July 4.

Ryan Howard steps in to bat against Washington on Sept. 28. After a slow start to the season, Howard's bat carried the team in September.

MICHAEL PEREZ / Staff Photographer

Adam Eaton, who wound up in the minors in the second year of his 3-year, $24.5 million contract, is heckled at the July 12 game.

Speedster Greg Golson is greeted by Scott Eyre after scoring the go-ahead run against the Braves on Sept. 22.

Shane Victorino wraps up Chris Coste, who singled him in to give the Phillies an 8-7, 13-inning win over the Mets on Aug. 26. The Mets had led the game, 7-0.

Eric Bruntlett filled in at shortstop for a month when Jimmy Rollins was hurt and often was a late defensive replacement in left.

Jayson Werth scores in the first game of a Sept. 14 doubleheader when the Phils capped a four-game sweep of the Brewers.

Shane Victorino leaps into the arms of Jayson Werth after knocking in the winning run against the Mets on July 4.

JERRY LODRIGUSS / Staff Photographer

Ryan Howard, always an adventure on defense, pulls down a popup against the Braves on Sept. 22.

RON CORTES / Staff Photographer

YONG KIM / Staff Photographer

Phillies catcher Chris Coste tags out the Braves'
Martin Prado on Sept. 24.

DAVID MAIALETTI / Staff Photographer

Charlie Manuel chats with general manager Pat Gillick
before a game in May.

Shane Victorino returns to the dugout after scoring the NL East-winning run on Pedro Feliz' eighth-inning double Sept. 27.

Chase Utley tags out the Nationals' Kory Casto on a seventh-inning doubleplay in the division-clinching win.

Brad Lidge celebrates after a doubleplay started by Jimmy Rollins clinched the NL East title.

Pat Burrell embraces Ryan Howard during the NL East championship celebration.

Brett Myers, whose strong second half helped win the division, sprays champagne after the season's final game.

Fireworks fly over Citizens Bank Park after Phillies won the NL East title that at one point was the Mets' for the taking.

Regular Season Key Moments

Opening Day jitters
March 31: Nationals 11, Phillies 6

Reliever Tom Gordon blows up in the ninth inning, allowing five runs in just one-third of an inning, spoiling a Phillies comeback. Chase Utley and Jimmy Rollins had homered in the seventh inning to tie the game at 6-6. Brett Myers gets the starting nod over Cole Hamels and allows four runs in five innings.

Sprain, no gain
April 8: Phillies 5, Mets 2

The Phillies win the first of a three-game series with the Mets at Shea Stadium but lose shortstop Jimmy Rollins, who sprains an ankle on a fake pickoff attempt in the eighth inning. Jamie Moyer earned his first win of the season but the Phillies struggle the rest of the series without Rollins, losing 8-2 in Game 2 and 4-3 in Game 3. Rollins does not return until May 9.

Pat the Sizzling Bat
April 23: Brewers 5, Phillies 4

Pat Burrell, hitting .351, continues his red-hot April with his eighth homer of the season, a solo shot in the sixth inning to take a 4-3 lead. But Cole Hamels gives up a two-run homer to Prince Fielder in the eighth. Burrell ends the month with a .326 batting average, eight homers and 24 RBI.

MVP Chase
April 24: Phillies 3, Brewers 1

The Phillies' line of succession for the NL MVP award seems right on pace as Chase Utley follows in the footsteps of Ryan Howard (2006) and Jimmy Rollins (2007) by going 3-for-4 to raise his batting average to .385. He would finish the month with 10 homers, 21 RBI, and a .352 average.

RON CORTES / Staff Photographer

Howard hits bottom
May 7: Phillies 5, Diamondbacks 4

Ryan Howard's batting average drops to a season-low .163 after he goes 0-for-4 with three strikeouts. Reliever J.C. Romero gets the win and Pedro Feliz hits a two-run home run. Howard's horrid start no doubt contributed to his omission from the NL All-Star team, but a torrid September would put him into the thick of the NL MVP race.

First place, then a struggle
June 1: Phillies, 7, Marlins 5

Down 5-1 in the third inning, the Phillies rally behind Chase Utley's homer and Pat Burrell's two-run double to take over first place in the NL East. But Utley would later struggle in June, going 0–for-24, and was taken out of the starting lineup for the first time on June 21.

Myers demoted to minors
July 1

Brett Myers, who was the Phillies' Opening Day starter and ace of the staff, is optioned to the Lehigh Valley IronPigs. Myers had a record of 3-9 with a 5.84 ERA. In his last start on June 27 against the Rangers, he gave up five earned runs over two innings as the Phillies lost, 8-7. How bad was he? Myers earned just one win (on May 30 against the Marlins) from April 17 until his demotion.

Rollins misses the bus
July 24: Mets 3, Phillies 1

Manager Charlie Manuel benches Jimmy Rollins for arriving late in the loss at Shea Stadium, which left the Phillies out of first place in the National League East for the first time since May 31. It was the second time

this season that Manuel benched him. He also did so on June 5 after the shortstop failed to run out a fly ball against Cincinnati. "Well, we're not going to agree on this one," said Rollins, who left the team hotel in Manhattan about 10 minutes after the team bus left for Shea Stadium. Manuel called a team meeting the next day.

Myers' triumphant return
July 29: Phillies 3, Nationals 1

Brett Myers' return from the minors was shaky, allowing five walks in five innings in a 6-3 loss to the Mets on July 23. He pitches brilliantly in his next start against the Nationals, allowing four hits, one unearned run and only one walk over seven innings to earn the victory.

Howard's incredible September
Sept. 11: Phillies 6, Brewers 3

In the first inning of a crucial four-game series with the Brewers, Ryan Howard hits a two-run homer to give the Phillies the lead. Howard finishes 2-for-3 with three RBI. In September, he has 11 homers and 32 RBI … maybe enough to earn a second MVP award.

Phils sweep Brewers
Sept. 14: Phillies 6, Brewers 1

Brett Myers pitches a two-hitter in the second game of a day/night doubleheader sweep of the Brewers. Pat Burrell hits a home run and Shane Victorino goes 4-for-4. Myers' win caps off a four-game sweep that moves the Phillies into a tie for the NL wild card and closes the Mets' lead in the NL East to one game.

Phillies regain first place
Sept. 20: Phillies 3, Marlins 2

After being pummeled by the Marlins, 14-8, the night before, the Phillies fight back to win behind Joe Blanton, who strikes out nine in five innings. The Phillies move back into first place with the victory — their eighth in nine games. They would not give up first place again.

Lidge closes out season
Sept. 27: Phillies 4, Nationals 3

Brad Lidge caps off a perfect season and clinches the NL East title with his 41st consecutive save. Jimmy Rollins makes a sliding grab up the middle with the bases loaded, and flips the ball to Chase Utley to start the game-ending doubleplay.

— *Chuck Bausman and Josh Schrager*

Ryan Howard welcomes home Carlos Ruiz and Cole Hamels after they scored on Chase Utley's two-out double in the third inning to give Hamels all the runs he would need to beat the Brewers, 3-1, in Game 1.

JERRY LODRIGUSS / Staff Photographer

CHAPTER FOUR

The NLDS

PHILS HAVE UNFINISHED BUSINESS
AFTER THE 2007 PLAYOFFS,
AND MILWAUKEE IS THE FIRST TO PAY.

BY TODD ZOLECKI

THE PHILLIES CELEBRATED their National League East championship in 2007 like a team that hadn't made the playoffs since 1993. They laughed. They hugged. They sprayed champagne and drank beers.

They partied like it couldn't end.

Except that it did end six days later when the Colorado Rockies swept the Phillies in the National League Division Series to leave a bitter taste in their mouths.

They were determined not to let it happen again.

First they had to beat the Milwaukee Brewers in the NLDS. The Brewers limped into the postseason after the Phillies swept them in a four-game series Sept. 11-14 at Citizens Bank Park, but they were in and had lefthander CC Sabathia, who just happened to be the hottest pitcher on the planet, pitching in Game 2 and a potential Game 5.

SERIES SUMMARY

Game 1		R	H	E
	Brewers	1	4	1
	Phillies	**3**	**4**	**1**

Game 2				
	Brewers	2	3	0
	Phillies	**5**	**9**	**1**

Game 3				
	Phillies	1	9	0
	Brewers	**4**	**11**	**0**

Game 4				
	Phillies	**6**	**10**	**0**
	Brewers	2	8	0

But while the Brewers were thrilled to make the playoffs for the first time since 1982, the Phillies entered the playoffs with a focus they lacked in 2007.

They weren't just happy to be there.

They came to win.

It showed up immediately in Game 1 on Oct. 1 at Citizens Bank Park. Cole Hamels had retired the first nine batters he faced when the Phillies stepped to the plate in the bottom of the third inning in a scoreless tie.

Carlos Ruiz, who hadn't hit much during the regular season, ripped a leadoff single to centerfield

The rays of the setting sun peek through the stands at Citizens Bank Park during the opening game of the Division Series.

and Hamels reached on an error to put runners on first and second with no outs. After Jimmy Rollins flied out and Jayson Werth struck out, Chase Utley ripped a line drive to center. The Brewers' Mike Cameron, one of the better defensive centerfielders in baseball, took a poor route to the ball. By the time he recovered, he got his glove on the ball but couldn't hold it as the Phillies took a 2-0 lead. Utley also eventually scored.

That was all Hamels needed. He threw eight shutout innings in a 3-1 victory.

"Vintage Cole," lefthander Jamie Moyer said. "The way he threw, the way he acted, the way he carried himself on the mound, his presence, I think was good."

But as much fun as Game 1 was, it couldn't match the excitement of Game 2. Not even close.

The Brewers took a 1-0 lead in the first inning, but all hell broke loose for Sabathia and the Brewers in the second. Werth and Pedro Feliz hit back-to-back doubles to tie the game. Sabathia then faced Myers

in an unforgettable at-bat with Feliz at third and two outs.

Myers had hit just .069 (4-for-58) in 2008, which ranked 58th out of 64 pitchers with at least 30 at-bats. But he impressively worked a nine-pitch walk, with fans cheering louder and louder every time he fouled off a pitch or Sabathia threw another ball.

They roared even louder when he went to first. "I know I'm a terrible hitter, but I really can't explain it," Myers said. "It was like one of those freakish things." The importance of Myers' at-bat cannot be understated. He not only made Sabathia throw nine pitches to him in the second inning, he made him throw 10 more to him in the fourth inning. His at-bat in the fourth ultimately resulted in a fly out to center, but Myers forced the hottest pitcher in baseball to throw 19 of his 98 pitches. Sabathia, who was making his fourth consecutive start on short rest, followed his long battle with Myers in the second inning with a quick four-pitch walk to Rollins to load the bases.

Brad Lidge gave Phillies fans some anxious moments in the ninth inning of Game 1, allowing a run and putting the tying runs on second and third before striking out Corey Hart to end it.

YONG KIM / Staff Photographer

"I don't think it frustrated me," Sabathia said.

Four pitches later, Shane Victorino smacked a 1-2 cutter into the leftfield stands for the first grand slam in Phillies postseason history. "Wow, did that really just happen?" Victorino said.

The crowd went crazy as the Phillies beat the Brewers in Game 2, 5-2. The Phillies needed just one more win to reach their first National League Championship Series since 1993.

That victory wouldn't come in Game 3 as the Brewers beat the Phillies on Oct. 4 at Miller Park, 4-1. Instead it came the next day with a 6-2 victory in Game 4.

Rollins hit a leadoff homer to rightfield in the first inning to make it 1-0. Victorino was on third with two outs in the third inning when Brewers righthander Jeff Suppan intentionally walked Ryan Howard to face Pat Burrell. It made some sense. Howard is a lefthanded hitter and Burrell is a righthanded hitter, so it put Burrell up against the righthanded Suppan. But Burrell had hit .454 (10-for-22) with two doubles, three home runs and eight RBI in his career against Suppan, including a second-inning single down the rightfield line. He also walked six times.

Burrell made the Brewers regret their decision. He crushed a 2-2 fastball to leftfield for a three-run homer to make it 4-0. Werth followed with a homer to left-center to make it 5-0.

The Phillies held on to win, clinching their first NLCS appearance in 15 years.

They had extended the party a little longer.

Rollins, soaked in champagne, his eyes burning from the alcohol, stood in the middle of the visitors' clubhouse at Miller Park and recalled a conversation he had with then-manager Larry Bowa when the Phillies closed Veterans Stadium in 2003.

" 'This is the house you helped build,' " Rollins said he told Bowa. " 'The one across the street is going to be the one that we build.' This is one step in the right direction."

They needed to make more magic in the playoffs to make Citizens Bank Park the House that Rollins and Utley and Howard and Hamels Built. And fortunately for Rollins, the Phillies were just getting started.

"We don't feel like we should be looking at anything less than a World Series," Rollins said. "And that's a World Series win. It's a lot of work. It's not going to be easy, but we weren't geared just to get to the playoffs. We're geared to win. We haven't broken through anything yet. We've just stepped over one hurdle." ●

JERRY LODRIGUSS / Staff Photographer

Cole Hamels begins his remarkable postseason run by blanking the Brewers on two hits in eight innings of Game 1.

JERRY LODRIGUSS / Staff Photographer

The Brewers' bench doesn't have much to get excited about for most of Game 1.

Chase Utley hits a two-run double in the third inning of NLDS Game 1. He came around to score the Phils' only other run in their 3-1 victory.

YONG KIM / Staff Photographer

Brett Myers had nine- and 10-pitch at-bats in Game 2, and held the Brewers to two hits in seven innings.

Brewers ace CC Sabathia, pitching on short rest, wouldn't make it through the fourth inning in Game 2.

Phillies: NLDS by the Numbers

INDIVIDUAL HITTING STATS

Name	AB	R	H	2B	3B	HR	RBI	BB	AVG
Joe Blanton	3	0	0	0	0	0	0	0	.000
Eric Bruntlett	1	0	1	0	0	0	0	0	1.000
Pat Burrell	12	2	3	0	0	2	4	2	.250
Greg Dobbs	5	0	3	0	0	0	0	0	.600
Pedro Feliz	13	1	3	1	0	0	1	0	.231
Cole Hamels	2	1	0	0	0	0	0	0	.000
Ryan Howard	11	1	2	1	0	0	1	5	.182
Geoff Jenkins	1	0	0	0	0	0	0	0	.000
Jamie Moyer	1	0	0	0	0	0	0	0	.000
Brett Myers	2	1	1	0	0	0	0	1	.500
Jimmy Rollins	16	2	6	2	0	1	1	1	.375
Carlos Ruiz	14	1	1	0	0	0	0	1	.071
Matt Stairs	2	0	0	0	0	0	0	0	.000
Chase Utley	15	1	2	1	0	0	2	2	.133
Shane Victorino	14	2	5	3	0	1	5	3	.357
Jayson Werth	16	3	5	3	1	1	1	0	.313
Team totals	**128**	**15**	**32**	**11**	**1**	**5**	**15**	**15**	**.250**

INDIVIDUAL PITCHING STATS

Name	W-L	ERA	G	SV	ER	H	BB	SO	IP
Joe Blanton	1-0	1.50	1	0	1	5	0	7	6.0
Clay Condrey	0-0	9.00	1	0	1	1	2	1	1.0
Chad Durbin	0-0	0.00	1	0	0	3	0	1	0.2
Scott Eyre	0-0	9.00	1	0	1	3	0	1	1.0
Cole Hamels	1-0	0.00	1	0	0	2	1	9	8.0
Brad Lidge	0-0	3.00	3	2	1	3	1	4	3.0
Ryan Madson	0-0	2.25	3	0	1	3	0	2	4.0
Jamie Moyer	0-1	4.50	1	0	2	4	3	3	4.0
Brett Myers	1-0	2.57	1	0	2	2	3	4	7.0
J.C. Romero	0-0	0.00	1	0	0	0	0	0	0.1
Team totals	**3-1**	**2.31**	**4**	**2**	**9**	**26**	**10**	**32**	**35.0**

Brewers: NLDS by the Numbers

INDIVIDUAL HITTING STATS

Name	AB	R	H	2B	3B	HR	RBI	BB	AVG
Ryan Braun	16	0	5	2	0	2	2	0	.313
Dave Bush	1	0	0	0	0	0	0	0	.000
Mike Cameron	13	3	2	0	0	0	0	3	.154
Craig Counsell	12	0	2	0	0	0	1	0	.167
Ray Durham	8	2	1	0	0	0	0	1	.125
Prince Fielder	14	1	1	0	0	1	2	2	.071
Yovani Gallardo	1	0	0	0	0	0	0	0	.000
Tony Gwynn	3	0	1	0	0	0	0	0	.333
Bill Hall	8	1	2	0	0	0	0	1	.250
J.J. Hardy	14	2	6	1	0	0	2	2	.429
Corey Hart	13	0	3	0	0	0	0	1	.231
Jason Kendall	14	0	2	0	0	0	1	0	.143
Brad Nelson	2	0	0	0	0	0	0	0	.000
CC Sabathia	2	0	0	0	0	0	0	0	.000
Carlos Villanueva	1	0	1	0	0	0	0	0	1.000
Rickie Weeks	4	0	0	0	0	0	0	0	.000
Team totals	**126**	**9**	**26**	**3**	**0**	**1**	**8**	**10**	**.206**

INDIVIDUAL PITCHING STATS

Name	W-L	ERA	G	SV	ER	H	BB	SO	IP
Dave Bush	1-0	1.69	1	0	1	5	0	3	5.1
Eric Gagne	0-0	0.00	2	0	0	1	0	1	2.0
Yovani Gallardo	0-1	0.00	2	0	0	4	5	4	7.0
Seth McClung	0-0	0.00	1	0	0	2	3	1	2.0
Guillermo Mota	0-0	5.40	2	0	1	2	0	0	1.2
Manny Parra	0-0	0.00	2	0	0	2	1	3	2.1
CC Sabathia	0-1	12.27	1	0	5	6	4	5	3.2
Mitch Stetter	0-0	0.00	3	0	0	0	0	2	1.1
Jeff Suppan	0-1	15.00	1	0	5	6	2	3	3.0
Salomon Torres	0-0	0.00	2	1	0	4	0	1	2.0
Carlos Villanueva	0-0	0.00	2	0	0	0	0	3	3.2
Team totals	**1-3**	**3.18**	**4**	**1**	**12**	**32**	**15**	**26**	**34.0**

Citizens Bank Park erupts after Shane Victorino's second-inning grand slam that doomed the Brewers.

RON CORTES / Staff Photographer

Jimmy Rollins' throw over the Brewers' Rickie Weeks isn't in time to complete a doubleplay in the eighth inning of Game 2.

Carlos Ruiz completes a doubleplay with a throw to first in the opening inning of Game 2.

Shane Victorino gestures to fans after hitting the first grand slam in Phillies postseason history during the second inning of Game 2.

RON CORTES / Staff Photographer

From left, Pat Burrell, Chase Utley and Jayson Werth reflect the Phils' mood in the ninth inning of their Game 3 loss.

Jimmy Rollins is tagged out by the Brewers' Eric Gagne during Game 3.

Game 3 starter Jamie Moyer's control problems led to two first-inning runs for the Brewers, all they would need.

Ever wonder what it feels like to foul a ball off your foot? Shane Victorino's face provides the answer in Game 3.

RON CORTES / Staff Photographer

**Jimmy Rollins
strikes out**
to lead off Game 3
in Milwaukee.

DAVID MAIALETTI /
Staff Photographer

Ryan Howard removes his hat for the national anthem before Game 3 in Milwaukee. It would be the Phils' only loss of the series.

Reliever Scott Eyre allows Brewers' final run in their lone victory.

The Brewers' Mike Cameron, after going from first to third on Bill Hall's single in the fifth inning of Game 3.

Pat Burrell follows through on the swing that launched a three-run homer to put Phils in command of Game 4.

Joe Blanton, acquired from Oakland in a July trade, pitches the clinching Game 4 victory.

RON CORTES / Staff Photographer

High-stepping Jimmy Rollins greets Jayson Werth after Werth's and Pat Burrell's back-to-back jacks in Game 4.

Jimmy Rollins' leadoff homer in the first inning gives the Phils the lead for good in the clincher.

MICHAEL PEREZ / Staff Photographer

DAVID MAIALETTI / Staff Photographer

Pat Burrell high-fives teammates after his second homer
in Game 4 helped seal the 6-2 win.

RON CORTES / Staff Photographer

Jayson Werth and Charlie Manuel yuk it up during
the Game 4 clincher.

Joe Blanton displays the form that held the Brewers to five hits and one run in six innings of Game 4.

Second baseman Chase Utley snatches Prince Fielder's line drive to end Brewers' eighth inning in Game 4.

Manager Charlie Manuel watches the eighth-inning action from the dugout in Game 4.

Perfect reliever Brad Lidge and catcher Carlos Ruiz embrace after Jason Kendall's groundout sends the Phils into the National League Championship Series.

RON CORTES / Staff Photographer

RON CORTES / Staff Photographer

Key Player: Shane Victorino

Centerfielder Shane Victorino was the man of the moment as the Phillies beat the Milwaukee Brewers in the National League Division Series.

Victorino broke open Game 2 by blasting a grand slam in the second inning off the Brewers' ace, CC Sabathia, sending the crowd at Citizens Bank Park into a frenzy. It was the first postseason grand slam in Phillies history. The Phillies won, 5-2, and finished off Milwaukee in four games as Victorino batted .357 in the series.

It's time for a group hug in Milwaukee after the Phillies dispose of the Brewers in Game 4 of the best-of-five NLDS.

DAVID MAIALETTI / Staff Photographer

CHAPTER FIVE

The NLCS

AGAINST A SOMBER BACKDROP
OF PERSONAL LOSSES, PHILLIES TAKE
CARE OF BUSINESS VS. DODGERS

BY PAUL HAGEN

CHARLIE MANUEL had a secret.

Phillies fans, and there were a legion of them by now, may have been tingling in anticipation of the National League Championship Series, the first for their team in 15 years.

Present: The Los Angeles Dodgers were the National League's hottest team, featuring electric — and eccentric — superstar Manny Ramirez. Past: The matchup also evoked memories of great postseason clashes of 1977 and 1978 and 1983, of Black Friday and Burt Hooton being jeered off the mound and Davey Lopes just beating Larry Bowa's throw at first. Or did he?

For one of the few times in his life, though, baseball wasn't uppermost on the Phillies manager's mind. He had learned a few days earlier that his mother, 87-year-old June Manuel, had been hospitalized back in Virginia.

They were close. When Manuel was 18, his father took his own life. That left the high school senior in charge of a family that included 11 children. More than four decades later, Manuel and his mother still were speaking several times a week; she often gave him tips on managing that he pretended to accept.

The manager kept all that to himself, though. So when Game 1 got started under unseasonably warm South Philadelphia skies at Citizens Bank Park on the

SERIES SUMMARY

Game 1

	R	H	E
Dodgers	2	7	1
Phillies	**3**	**7**	**0**

Game 2

	R	H	E
Dodgers	5	8	1
Phillies	**8**	**11**	**1**

Game 3

	R	H	E
Phillies	2	7	0
Dodgers	**7**	**10**	**0**

Game 4

	R	H	E
Phillies	**7**	**12**	**1**
Dodgers	5	11	0

Game 5

	R	H	E
Phillies	**5**	**8**	**0**
Dodgers	1	7	3

night of Oct. 9, the smart money was drifting toward the Dodgers and the focus was on the pitching match-up between veteran Dodgers righthander Derek Lowe and the Phillies' 24-year-old lefty, Cole Hamels.

Los Angeles grabbed an early 2-0 lead. Lowe was mastering the Phillies hitters, using his heavy sinker to induce ground ball after harmless ground ball.

In the sixth, the Phillies got their break. Shane Victorino led off with a grounder to shortstop. Rafael Furcal made a wild throw and Victorino ended up on second.

Lowe would later say that the error hadn't upset him. Still, that seemed to be the most obvious explanation for why an experienced big-game pitcher who had been staying down in the strike zone the entire game would suddenly start leaving the ball up. He did it with his first pitch to Chase Utley and the second baseman hammered the ball into the rightfield seats to tie the score. Two batters later he did it to Pat Burrell, and the leftfielder knocked it out to left.

That accounted for all the runs the Phillies would get, but it was enough as Hamels went seven strong innings to help preserve the 3-2 win.

Manuel's private life became public the next afternoon, before Game 2, after he concluded a meeting with his coaches and got the call telling him his mother had passed away. Stoically, he went through his normal pregame routine and indicated his intention of staying with the team. That surprised nobody who remembered that, on the day of his father's funeral, he had insisted on playing in his team's scheduled game ... and homered.

That was the prelude to one of the strangest, most emotionally charged playoff games ever.

On the field, it was all Phillies. Gifted Dodgers righthander Chad Billingsley lasted just 2⅓ innings, giving up eight runs. Starting pitcher Brett Myers, a self-described "terrible hitter," had three hits, drove in three runs and scored twice.

And centerfielder Shane Victorino had a day to remember. He had a single, a triple and four RBI. He made a leaping catch at the wall to help snuff out a Dodgers rally in the seventh. He was interviewed on national television after the 8-5 win was in the books.

Then, as he entered the clubhouse, he was ushered into the office of travel director Frank Coppenbarger. There his father, Mike, broke the news that his paternal grandmother had died earlier that day in Hawaii. Irene Victorino was 82.

DAVID MAIALETTI / Staff Photographer

Dodgers manager Joe Torre exchanges pleasantries with Charlie Manuel before Game 1.

The Phillies had a commanding lead of two games to none in the best-of-seven series, but nobody felt like celebrating as the players packed for their charter flight to Los Angeles.

Sorrow gave way to anger in Game 3 at majestic Dodger Stadium. Myers had thrown a pitch behind Ramirez two days earlier. It didn't seem like a big thing at the time. Apparently it was. Dodgers starter Hiroki Kuroda brushed back Utley in the first inning. When he sailed one over Victorino's head in the third, both benches emptied. Victorino pointed at Kuroda, clearly pantomiming that while it's all right to throw at somebody's ribs, above the shoulders is out of bounds. The umpires issued a warning to both benches.

Shane Victorino gives Chase Utley a big hand after Utley's two-run homer in the sixth inning of Game 1 wiped out the Dodgers' 2-0 lead.

YONG KIM / Staff Photographer

Fans in the leftfield stands at Citizens Bank Park try to get their hands on Pat Burrell's home-run ball in Game 1.

That couldn't overshadow the concern after veteran lefthander Jamie Moyer lasted just 1⅓ innings and gave up six runs. The Dodgers won easily, 7-2. It was Moyer's second straight subpar outing in the postseason and if the series went the distance, it would be his turn to start the decisive Game 7.

Dodgers manager Joe Torre had chosen to bring Lowe back on short rest for Game 4. That would have made him available for Game 7 on full rest. Manuel had taken the opposite approach. Joe Blanton, the midseason pickup from the Oakland Athletics, would start Game 4.

With Barbra Streisand among the celebrities in attendance, Blanton was good enough. But the real heroics were provided by Victorino, who was now being treated as a villain by the normally chilled-out Chavez Ravine crowd, and Matt Stairs.

The Dodgers were on the verge of evening the series at two games each, leading 5-3 into the eighth when Victorino belted a two-run homer off Cory Wade to tie the score.

With two outs and a runner on first, Stairs stepped to the plate as a pinch-hitter. When he was acquired from the Blue Jays for lefthander Fabio Castro on Aug. 30, the deal was considered something of an afterthought. Stairs made the move look positively prescient. He slammed a fastball from Dodgers closer Jonathan Broxton halfway up the rightfield pavilion.

"I'm not going to lie, I try to hit home runs and that's it," Stairs said. "My whole career, my approach has been to try to hit the ball out of the ballpark. In batting practice, I'm trying to hit the ball out of the ballpark. It's fun. The biggest thing is to get up there and see how far you can hit the ball."

That's not exactly Ted Williams on the science of hitting, but the Phillies weren't going to complain.

Brad Lidge nailed down the 7-5 win with a four-out save and the Phillies were one win away from their first World Series appearance since 1993.

After yet another off day, this one dictated by

Manny Ramirez and his Dodgers teammates don't seem to be enjoying the view in the ninth inning of Game 1.

Phillies first baseman Ryan Howard gets handcuffed by Andre Ethier's Game 1 single.

Cole Hamels, who would go on to win the NLCS MVP award, tosses the first pitch of Game 1.

Pat Burrell trots home after his solo shot in the sixth inning of the NLCS opener — right on the heels of Chase Utley's two-run homer — gave the Phillies a come-from-behind, 3-2 win over the Dodgers.

television, the stage was set for Game 5 on Oct. 15. It turned out to be anticlimactic. The drama ended early when Billingsley again couldn't complete even three innings. The Phillies cruised to a 5-1 win behind Hamels, who was voted NLCS Most Valuable Player.

The traditional celebration erupted in the tiny visitors' clubhouse at Dodger Stadium. Phillies chairman Bill Giles, the honorary NL president, presented the Warren Giles Trophy to Manuel. Giles became teary-eyed; the award is named after his late father.

Dodgers manager Joe Torre fought his way into Manuel's tiny office to offer his congratulations. "You're a good man," he said to Manuel.

Now all the Phillies could do was wait to see whether they'd be playing the Boston Red Sox or the Tampa Bay Rays in the World Series. Most of the traveling party would fly back to Philadelphia.

Not Manuel. He had a private jet waiting that would take him directly to Virginia. He had a funeral to attend. ●

Shane Victorino and Dodgers pitcher Derek Lowe meet by accident at first during Game 1.

In a familiar pose, flawless reliever Brad Lidge exults after saving Game 1.

Manny Ramirez, who batted .533 in the NLCS, is frustrated after lining out in Game 1.

Phillies: NLCS by the Numbers

INDIVIDUAL HITTING STATS

Name	AB	R	H	2B	3B	HR	RBI	BB	AVG
Joe Blanton	2	0	0	0	0	0	0	0	.000
Eric Bruntlett	2	0	0	0	0	0	0	1	.000
Pat Burrell	18	1	6	0	0	1	3	1	.333
Chris Coste	1	0	1	0	0	0	0	0	1.000
Greg Dobbs	6	2	3	1	0	0	0	1	.500
Pedro Feliz	13	0	2	0	0	0	1	1	.154
Cole Hamels	5	0	1	0	0	0	0	0	.200
Ryan Howard	20	4	6	1	0	0	2	3	.300
Geoff Jenkins	1	0	0	0	0	0	0	0	.000
Brett Myers	3	2	3	0	0	0	3	0	1.000
Jimmy Rollins	21	4	3	0	0	1	1	2	.143
Carlos Ruiz	16	3	5	1	0	0	1	1	.313
Matt Stairs	1	1	1	0	0	1	2	0	1.000
So Taguchi	4	0	0	0	0	0	0	0	.000
Chase Utley	17	4	6	2	0	1	3	6	.353
Shane Victorino	18	2	4	0	1	1	6	2	.222
Jayson Werth	21	2	4	1	0	0	0	1	.190
Team totals	**169**	**25**	**45**	**6**	**1**	**5**	**22**	**19**	**.266**

INDIVIDUAL PITCHING STATS

Name	W-L	ERA	G	SV	ER	H	BB	SO	IP
Joe Blanton	0-0	5.40	1	0	3	7	4	4	5
Clay Condrey	0-0	0.00	1	0	0	0	1	0	0.2
Chad Durbin	0-0	4.50	3	0	1	3	2	2	2
Scott Eyre	0-0	0.00	2	0	0	0	1	0	1.1
Cole Hamels	2-0	1.93	2	0	3	11	5	13	14
J.A. Happ	0-0	3.00	1	0	1	4	2	2	3
Brad Lidge	0-0	0.00	4	3	0	2	2	6	4.1
Ryan Madson	1-0	0.00	4	0	0	4	1	4	5
Jamie Moyer	0-1	40.50	1	0	6	6	0	2	1.1
Brett Myers	1-0	9.00	1	0	5	6	4	6	5
J.C. Romero	0-0	0.00	3	0	0	0	3	3	2.1
Team totals	**4-1**	**3.89**	**5**	**3**	**19**	**43**	**25**	**42**	**44.0**

Dodgers: NLCS by the Numbers

INDIVIDUAL HITTING STATS

Name	AB	R	H	2B	3B	HR	RBI	BB	AVG
Angel Berroa	1	0	0	0	0	0	0	0	.000
Chad Billingsley	1	0	0	0	0	0	0	0	.000
Casey Blake	19	2	5	0	0	1	2	2	.263
Blake DeWitt	13	0	1	0	1	0	5	1	.077
Andre Ethier	22	4	5	1	0	0	0	1	.227
Rafael Furcal	19	5	4	0	0	1	1	3	.211
Nomar Garciaparra	7	0	3	0	0	0	1	1	.429
Matt Kemp	15	1	5	1	0	0	0	4	.333
Jeff Kent	8	0	0	0	0	0	0	0	.000
Hiroki Kuroda	3	0	0	0	0	0	0	0	.000
James Loney	16	0	7	2	0	0	2	3	.438
Derek Lowe	4	0	1	0	0	0	0	0	.250
Russell Martin	17	3	2	0	0	0	1	3	.118
Pablo Ozuna	1	0	0	0	0	0	0	0	.000
Juan Pierre	3	1	2	1	0	0	0	0	.667
Manny Ramirez	15	4	8	2	0	2	7	7	.533
Team totals	**165**	**20**	**43**	**7**	**1**	**4**	**19**	**25**	**.261**

INDIVIDUAL PITCHING STATS

Name	W-L	ERA	G	SV	ER	H	BB	SO	IP
Joe Beimel	0-0	0.00	3	0	0	0	2	0	0.2
Chad Billingsley	0-2	18.00	2	0	10	12	7	9	5
Jonathan Broxton	0-0	3.86	2	0	1	3	1	2	2.1
Clayton Kershaw	0-0	4.50	2	0	1	1	2	1	2
Hong-Chi Kuo	0-0	3.00	3	0	1	2	0	3	3
Hiroki Kuroda	1-0	3.00	1	0	2	5	1	3	6
Derek Lowe	0-1	3.48	2	0	4	12	2	6	10.1
Greg Maddux	0-0	0.00	2	0	0	3	1	3	3
James McDonald	0-0	0.00	2	0	0	3	2	7	5.1
Chan Ho Park	0-0	0.00	4	0	0	1	1	1	1.2
Cory Wade	0-1	4.91	4	0	2	3	0	2	3.2
Team totals	**1-4**	**4.40**	**5**	**0**	**21**	**45**	**19**	**37**	**43.0**

Ryan Howard isn't quite sure that was a strike he saw after taking a called third in Game 2.

Phillies fans jeer Dodgers starting pitcher Chad Billingsley as he heads to the dugout after being removed from the game.

Brett Myers is as surprised as anyone after he got three hits and three RBI in Game 2.

Shane Victorino makes the play of the day in Game 2, leaping against the centerfield fence to rob Casey Blake.

YONG KIM / Staff Photographer

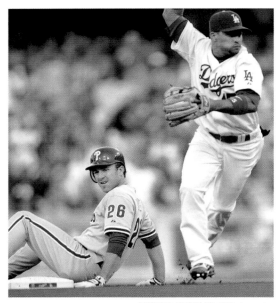

Chase Utley has just been tagged by Rafael Furcal on attempted steal of second in Game 3.

Shane Victorino has a few words for Hiroki Kuroda about a pitch that just missed his noggin in Game 3.

Pat Burrell, whose RBI double cut the Dodgers' lead to 7-2 in the seventh inning, tosses his helmet after being stranded.

YONG KIM / Staff Photographer

Shane Victorino is restrained after his exchange with Hiroki Kuroda led to a benches-clearing confrontation.

YONG KIM / Staff Photographer

Charlie Manuel heads off the field after Game 3 brouhaha.

YONG KIM / Staff Photographer

Dodgers coach Larry Bowa (remember him?) makes a pointed remark during the fracas.

Jimmy Rollins sails over
James Loney while
turning the doubleplay
that ended the fifth inning
of Game 4, but not before
the Dodgers scored twice
to take a 3-2 lead.

YONG KIM / Staff Photographer

The Phillies have a knack of winning games started by Joe Blanton, who got a no-decision in the Game 4 victory.

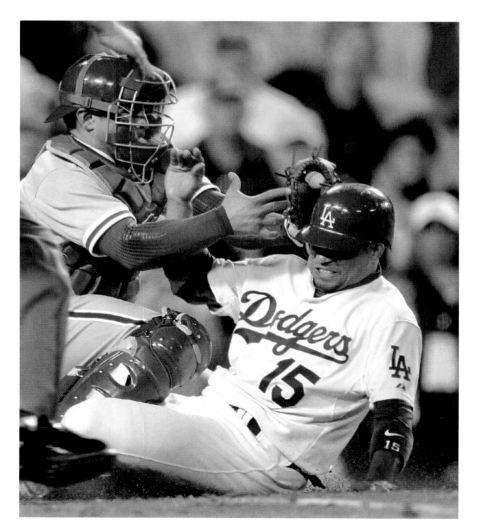

Ryan Howard is pumped up after scoring the tying run on a wild pitch in the fifth inning of Game 4.

Rafael Furcal crosses the plate ahead of the tag by Carlos Ruiz in Game 4.

Late-season acquisition Matt Stairs admires his pinch two-run homer that capped the Phils' four-run eighth inning in their 7-5, Game 4 win. At right, his teammates also enjoy it.

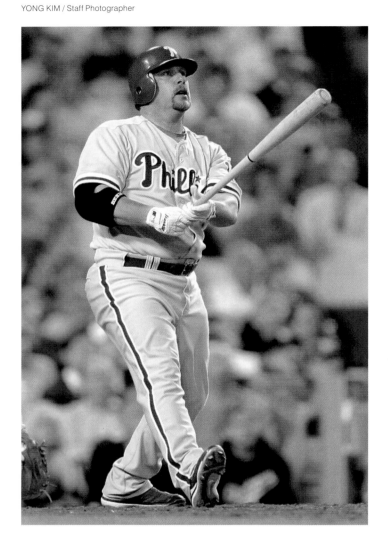

Chase Utley doubles Rafael Furcal off second base after snagging Russell Martin's line drive in the sixth inning of Game 4.

Shane Victorino's two-run homer in the eighth inning tied Game 4 ahead of Matt Stairs' game-winner.

Brad Lidge closes out Game 4 with a 1-2-3 ninth.

Jimmy Rollins, beating the tag on a steal of second, would go on to score the Phils' second run in their 5-1 victory in Game 5.

Jayson Werth has a few words with Rafael Furcal after being forced out at second in Game 5 doubleplay.

Ryan Howard drives in Jimmy Rollins with this third-inning single in Game 5.

Chase Utley scores from second on Rafael Furcal's throwing error to give the Phils a 4-0 lead in the fifth inning of Game 5.

Jimmy Rollins completes a fifth-inning doubleplay despite Matt Kemp's takeout slide.

Brad Lidge starts the NLCS celebration with Carlos Ruiz, who caught Nomar Garciaparra's foul pop for the final out.

YONG KIM / Staff Photographer

Carlos Ruiz reacts after catching a foul that ended the NLCS.

YONG KIM / Staff Photographer

Charlie Manuel poses with the Warren Giles Trophy that goes to the National League champion.

RON CORTES / Staff Photographer

Phillies uncork their emotions in the clubhouse after Game 5. It wasn't to be their last champagne shower.

The Phillies celebrate the National League pennant as if they hadn't won it in 15 years.
MICHAEL PEREZ / Staff Photographer

Key Player: Matt Stairs

Pinch-hitting specialist Matt Stairs was the man of the moment as the Phillies beat the Los Angeles Dodgers in the National League Championship Series.

After the Dodgers dominated Game 4 for seven innings, Shane Victorino tied it at 5-5 with a two-run homer in the eighth inning. Carlos Ruiz then singled with two outs and Stairs was sent up to pinch-hit for Ryan Madson. With flame-throwing closer Jonathan Broxton dealing for the Dodgers, Stairs took the first pitch for a strike. He ran the count to 3-1 when Broxton served him a letter-high fastball. The ball exploded off Stairs' bat and sailed into the rightfield seats for a two-run homer. It was Stairs' only at-bat of the series, and it gave the Phils a 7-5 victory and set up Cole Hamels' Game 5 gem to clinch it.

Several thousand Phillies fans pour into the street at Frankford near Cottman in the city's Mayfair section after the Phils beat the Dodgers.

After the first two games at Tampa Bay, the World Series is welcomed to Philadelphia with a big bang.

STEVEN M. FALK / Staff Photographer

CHAPTER SIX

The World Series

THE PHILS REACH THE PROMISED LAND, BUT NOT BEFORE A COUPLE OF DAYS ON NOAH'S ARK.

BY TODD ZOLECKI

BRAD LIDGE dropped to his knees and thrust his arms into the sky at 9:58 p.m. on Oct. 29.

Carlos Ruiz ripped off his mask and ran toward him.

They met just in front of the pitcher's mound at Citizens Bank Park, the first pieces of a celebratory pile Philadelphia had not seen since 1980.

Ryan Howard jumped in next. Then Geoff Jenkins. Then Jimmy Rollins. Then Chase Utley. Then everybody. Shane Victorino got there, with the Flyin' Hawaiian leaping high into the air before falling on his teammates, who were nothing more than a messy, blurry heap of red and white at that point. Lidge, who struck out Tampa Bay Rays pinchhitter Eric Hinske on an 0-2 slider to win Game 5 of the World Series, 4-3, had just made the Phillies World Series champions.

It had been 28 years since the Phillies ruled the world.

It had been 25 years since the city of Philadelphia celebrated its last title.

Droughts? Curses?

Gone.

"I grew up watching this silly team play," said Souderton native Jamie Moyer. "And now I'm standing in their clubhouse as a player, and we won a world championship."

SERIES SUMMARY

		R	H	E
Game 1	Phillies	3	8	1
	Rays	2	5	1
Game 2	Phillies	2	9	2
	Rays	**4**	**7**	**1**
Game 3	Rays	4	6	1
	Phillies	**5**	**7**	**1**
Game 4	Rays	2	5	2
	Phillies	**10**	**12**	**1**
Game 5	Rays	3	10	0
	Phillies	**4**	**8**	**1**

Chase Utley sets the tone early for the Phillies with this two-run homer in the first inning of Game 1.

MICHAEL PEREZ / Staff Photographer

Ryan Howard lines up to make a catch over the outstretched arms of Rays fans during Game 1 at Tropicana Field.

"I tell you what," Pat Burrell said. "It couldn't be sweeter. It's too much. It's too much."

Everybody had been hoping and praying and dreaming of this moment.

How would it feel?

Awesome.

Simply awesome.

The Phillies played in a memorable World Series, which will be remembered because Game 5 started on a Monday and finished on a Wednesday. Major League Baseball suspended Game 5 in the middle of the sixth inning Monday — just after the Rays tied the game in the top of the sixth — because of a cold, hard rain. Fans waited 46 hours for the series to resume, but not even Mother Nature could stop the Phillies this time.

And if Mother Nature could not stop the Phillies in 2008, the Mets, Brewers, Dodgers and Rays had no chance.

The Phillies opened their first World Series since 1993 in Tropicana Field in St. Petersburg, Fla., on Oct. 22. Cole Hamels, fresh off being named MVP of the National League Championship Series, held the Rays to two runs in seven innings in a 3-2 victory. His legend as a big-game pitcher grew.

"I knew he was good, but not that good," Rays third baseman Evan Longoria said. "He did what a No. 1 starter in the World Series is supposed to do."

Utley hit a two-run home run in the first inning to give the Phillies the early lead. He had tried to bunt on the first pitch from Rays lefthander Scott Kazmir, but fortunately for him the ball went foul.

"I guess it turned out pretty well," Utley said.

Ruiz knocked in the third run with a fielder's choice in the fourth. Ryan Madson pitched a perfect eighth inning in relief. Lidge, like always, picked up the save in the ninth.

The Phillies lost Game 2, 4-2, falling to 1-for-28

with runners in scoring position in the series. That was a cause of concern to outsiders who had seen great Philadelphia teams fall short in the past. But this team wasn't like those teams. This team had a special quality about it.

It never panicked. It always rose to the occasion.

The Phillies returned home to Citizens Bank Park to play Game 3 on Oct. 25. Rain delayed the first pitch 1 hour, 31 minutes, but every second the fans waited in the rain proved to be worth it as Ruiz chopped a ball down the third-base line with the bases loaded in the ninth inning to score the winning run in a 5-4 victory.

Rays lefthander J.P. Howell had hit Eric Bruntlett with a pitch to lead off the ninth. Right-hander Grant Balfour replaced Howell and threw a wild pitch. The ball hit off the backstop and straight back to Rays catcher Dioner Navarro, who threw to second.

"I started to break for second and turned to look back and saw the ball come back to him," Bruntlett said. "There was a moment there where I wasn't sure. I thought he maybe had a play on me at second base."

But Navarro's throw was wild and the ball wound up in centerfield as Bruntlett scampered to third. Balfour intentionally walked Shane Victorino and pinch-hitter Greg Dobbs to load the bases.

Rays manager Joe Maddon then brought in his infield. He brought in an extra infielder, too, right-fielder Ben Zobrist to play second base. That's when Ruiz chopped a ball down the third-base line. Longoria lunged and tried to flip it to the plate, but the throw sailed over Navarro's head.

There was no play. Bruntlett was safe.

The Phillies had won.

"I saw the ball go into the ground," Bruntlett said. "I knew it wasn't hit very hard, so I know I just have to high-tail it and go as hard as I can ... It's one of those deals where it kind of feels like everything is slow motion. I feel like I should be moving faster and I can't because you want to get there so quickly. It feels like a long 90 feet at that point."

Moyer, who had struggled in his first two postseason starts, allowed three runs in 6⅓ innings, throwing off a mound where Tim McGraw, the country-singing son of former Phillies closer Tug McGraw, spread some of his father's ashes before the game.

"I'm sure he thought it was going to be good luck," Moyer said. "And it turns out that it probably was. It's pretty cool."

The Phillies crushed the Rays in Game 4, 10-2. Ryan Howard hit a couple of home runs. Even pitcher Joe Blanton hit one. Blanton also allowed just four hits and two runs in six-plus innings to pick up the win. He improved to 2-0 with a 3.18 ERA in three starts in the postseason.

One more to go.

"Maybe there will be a greater appreciation, if it does happen," Moyer said. "I think sometimes the longer you wait for things, the more you appreciate things. And when you feel like things are earned ... I feel like I've earned a lot of things in my career. I don't feel like I've been given a whole lot, but I don't expect to be given a whole lot.

YONG KIM / Staff Photographer

Charlie Manuel doesn't have any answers in Game 2, which the Rays won by a 4-2 score.

"I would hate to use the word *assume*, but I feel like our fans are probably the same way. They've given their heart and soul and their hard-earned money to come out here and watch the games. But they've also supported us. And it's exciting because you feel like you're doing this thing together with a city. And I think that's pretty special."

Game 5 started on a Monday, with the Phillies taking a 2-0 lead in the first inning on a two-out single by Victorino. The Rays tied the game in the top of the sixth in unplayable conditions.

Could God really be telling Philadelphia that he didn't want them to win a championship?

No, not at all. Because when play resumed Wednesday, Geoff Jenkins, who hadn't had a hit since Sept. 28, hit a pinch-hit, leadoff double to right-centerfield. With the infield in, he scored on Jayson Werth's flare single to shallow centerfield to give the Phillies a 3-2 lead. The Rays made it 3-3 in the top of the seventh, but Pat Burrell, who had been hitless

Jayson Werth is doubled off first by Carlos Pena after Chase Utley's liner to right in the fifth inning of Game 2.

in 13 at-bats in the World Series, led off the seventh with a double to left-centerfield.

Bruntlett, pinch-running for Burrell, went to third on Victorino's grounder to second and scored on Pedro Feliz' single through a drawn-in infield to make it 4-3.

Now the Phillies just needed to hold it.

They did.

"It was deafening," Lidge said of the crowd on the final pitch to Hinske. "I just had to make sure I took a deep breath. I had to step back because my heart was going 100 miles per hour."

About an hour after the final out had been recorded, after the Phillies paraded their 2008 championship flag around the ballpark, after more than 45,000 fans sang Queen's "We Are the Champions," Rollins reflected on the moment. He had proclaimed the Phillies the team to beat in the National League East in 2007, and they were. He predicted 100 wins this year. They got 103. His next prediction?

"This is just the beginning." ●

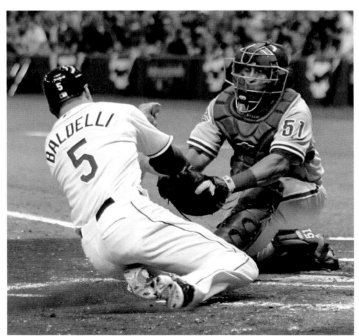

Carlos Ruiz holds the ball in this crash with Rocco Baldelli, out trying to score from second on B.J. Upton's RBI single in the second inning of Game 2.

Six-year-old Joshua Garcia waits for the rain to stop before Game 3, which was delayed for an hour-and-a-half.

Jamie Moyer playfully expresses his relief after Evan Longoria's fly to deep leftfield is caught in Game 3.

Ryan Howard gestures after he and Chase Utley hit back-to-back homers in the sixth inning of Game 3.

YONG KIM / Staff Photographer

Cole Hamels' Game 1 masterpiece in St. Pete gave him his fourth postseason win.

MICHAEL PEREZ / Staff Photographer

Rays third baseman Evan Longoria looks like he's ready to punch the next Phillies fan who calls him Eva.

Phillies: World Series by the Numbers

INDIVIDUAL HITTING STATS

Name	AB	R	H	2B	3B	HR	RBI	BB	AVG
Joe Blanton	3	1	1	0	0	1	1	0	.333
Eric Bruntlett	3	3	1	0	0	1	1	0	.333
Pat Burrell	14	0	1	1	0	0	1	5	.071
Chris Coste	4	0	0	0	0	0	0	0	.000
Greg Dobbs	3	0	1	0	0	0	0	1	.333
Pedro Feliz	18	0	6	0	0	0	2	1	.333
Cole Hamels	2	0	0	0	0	0	0	0	.000
Ryan Howard	21	3	6	1	0	3	6	3	.286
Geoff Jenkins	2	1	1	1	0	0	0	0	.500
Jamie Moyer	2	0	0	0	0	0	0	0	.000
Jimmy Rollins	22	4	5	2	0	0	0	1	.227
J.C. Romero	1	0	0	0	0	0	0	0	.000
Carlos Ruiz	16	2	6	2	0	1	3	4	.375
Matt Stairs	1	0	0	0	0	0	0	0	.000
Chase Utley	18	5	3	0	0	2	4	5	.167
Shane Victorino	20	1	5	0	0	0	2	1	.250
Jayson Werth	18	4	8	3	0	1	3	6	.444
Team totals	**168**	**24**	**44**	**10**	**0**	**9**	**23**	**27**	**.262**

INDIVIDUAL PITCHING STATS

Name	W-L	ERA	G	SV	ER	H	BB	SO	IP
Joe Blanton	1-0	3.00	1	0	2	4	2	7	6.0
Chad Durbin	0-0	0.00	2	0	0	1	1	0	0.2
Scott Eyre	0-0	0.00	2	0	0	0	0	1	0.2
Cole Hamels	1-0	2.77	2	0	4	10	3	8	13.0
Brad Lidge	0-0	0.00	2	2	0	1	0	3	2.0
Ryan Madson	0-0	4.91	4	0	2	3	0	6	3.2
Jamie Moyer	0-0	4.26	1	0	3	5	1	5	6.1
Brett Myers	0-1	3.86	1	0	3	7	3	2	7.0
J.C. Romero	2-0	0.00	4	0	0	2	0	4	4.2
Team totals	**4-1**	**2.86**	**5**	**2**	**14**	**33**	**10**	**36**	**44.0**

Rays: World Series by the Numbers

INDIVIDUAL HITTING STATS

Name	AB	R	H	2B	3B	HR	RBI	BB	AVG
Willy Aybar	4	0	1	0	0	0	0	1	.250
Rocco Baldelli	6	1	1	0	0	1	1	1	.167
Jason Bartlett	14	1	3	0	0	0	2	2	.214
Carl Crawford	19	4	5	1	0	2	2	0	.263
Cliff Floyd	3	1	1	0	0	0	0	0	.333
Matt Garza	2	0	0	0	0	0	0	0	.000
Gabe Gross	3	0	0	0	0	0	2	0	.000
Eric Hinske	2	1	1	0	0	1	1	0	.500
Akinori Iwamura	19	1	5	1	0	0	1	1	.263
Scott Kazmir	2	0	0	0	0	0	0	0	.000
Evan Longoria	20	0	1	0	0	0	2	0	.050
Dioner Navarro	17	2	6	1	0	0	0	1	.353
Carlos Pena	17	1	2	1	0	0	2	3	.118
Andy Sonnanstine	1	0	1	0	0	0	0	0	1.000
B.J. Upton	20	3	5	0	0	0	1	0	.250
Ben Zobrist	7	0	1	0	0	0	0	1	.143
Team totals	**156**	**15**	**33**	**4**	**0**	**4**	**14**	**10**	**.212**

INDIVIDUAL PITCHING STATS

Name	W-L	ERA	G	SV	ER	H	BB	SO	IP
Grant Balfour	0-0	3.00	3	0	1	4	3	2	3.0
Chad Bradford	0-0	0.00	2	0	0	1	1	0	2.0
Matt Garza	0-0	6.00	1	0	4	6	2	7	6.0
J.P. Howell	0-2	7.71	3	0	2	2	1	5	2.1
Edwin Jackson	0-0	4.50	1	0	1	2	1	1	2.0
Scott Kazmir	0-1	4.50	2	0	5	10	10	9	10.0
Trever Miller	0-0	18.00	2	0	2	1	1	1	1.0
David Price	0-0	2.70	2	0	1	2	2	4	3.1
James Shields	1-0	0.00	1	0	0	7	2	4	5.2
Andy Sonnanstine	0-1	6.75	1	0	3	6	3	2	4.0
Dan Wheeler	0-0	6.75	3	0	2	3	1	3	2.2
Team totals	**1-4**	**4.50**	**5**	**0**	**21**	**44**	**27**	**38**	**42.0**

Carl Crawford reaches on Game 3 bunt after Jamie Moyer laid out and flipped the ball from his glove to Ryan Howard's bare hand. After the game, the ump said he blew the call.

Chase Utley leads off the sixth inning of Game 3 with a homer that Ryan Howard followed with one of his own as the Phils took a 4-1 lead en route to 5-4 victory.

Shane Victorino takes to the air to elude Grant Balfour's wild pitch in the ninth inning of Game 3.

Carlo Ruiz hits a bases-loaded dribbler to third base that knocks in the winning run of Game 3.

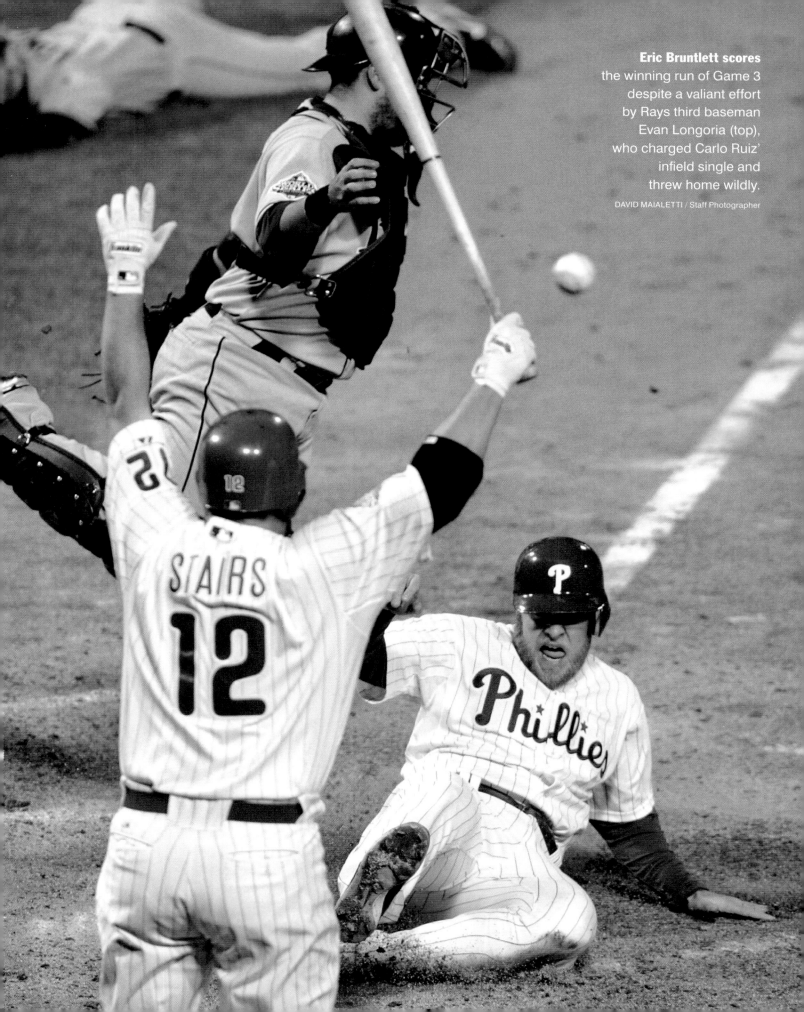

On another blown call, Jimmy Rollins is ruled safe after being tagged by Rays third baseman Evan Longoria on this first-inning rundown in Game 4. He went on to score the game's first run.

BARBARA JOHNSTON / Staff Photographer

MICHAEL PEREZ / Staff Photographer

DAVID MAIALETTI / Staff Photographer

Jayson Werth congratulates Ryan Howard, whose three-run homer in the fourth inning of Game 4 broke open a 2-1 Phillies lead.

RON CORTES / Staff Photographer

Phillies' Game 4 starter Joe Blanton hits the first home run of his career, and becomes the first pitcher to hit one in the World Series since 1974.

YONG KIM / Staff Photographer

Joe Blanton finds out what it's like to return to the dugout after a homer.

Pedro Feliz throws out Jason Bartlett in the fifth after the ball ricocheted off Joe Blanton.

117

MICHAEL PEREZ / Staff Photographer

Evan Longoria, hitless in the first four games, flips his bat after Game 4 strikeout.

BARBARA JOHNSTON / Staff Photographer

Jayson Werth's two-run homer in the eighth boosts the Game 4 lead to 8-2.

Shane Victorino watches his two-run single with two out in the first inning of Game 5.

Jayson Werth and Chase Utley high-five after scoring on Shane Victorino's clutch hit in the first inning.

Chase Utley takes one for the team in the first inning of Game 5.

JERRY LODRIGUSS / Staff Photographer

Jayson Werth can't pull down Carlos Pena's fourth-inning double in Game 5.

JERRY LODRIGUSS / Staff Photographer

Battling weather elements, Jimmy Rollins misses Rocco Baldelli's popup in the fourth inning ...

DAVID MAIALETTI / Staff Photographer

YONG KIM / Staff Photographer

Cole Hamels fouls a bunt attempt off the fingers of his pitching hand in the fourth inning of Game 5.

... but Chase Utley then erases Baldelli on a doubleplay.

YONG KIM / Staff Photographer

B.J. Upton scores on Carlos Pena's two-out single in the sixth inning to tie Game 5 before play was stopped.

MICHAEL PEREZ / Staff Photographer

A member of the grounds crew walks past the tarp that would stay on the field for a couple of days.

STEVEN M. FALK / Staff Photographer

Jimmy Rollins awaits a pitch on the infield dirt that the grounds crew tried to make playable.

Fans at Day 1 of Game 5 ended up with a reign delay.

RLD SERIES

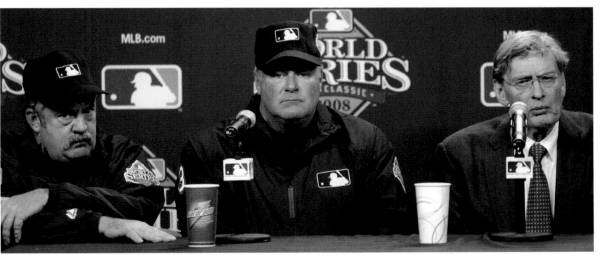

From left, umpires Tom Hallion and Tim Welke and commissioner Bud Selig announce that Game 5 would be suspended in the middle of the sixth inning.

When Game 5 resumed 46 hours later, the fans still had a sense of humor.

Rays second baseman Akinori Iwamura can't come up with Jayson Werth's bloop RBI single in the sixth.

Geoff Jenkins, who led off the resumed game with a pinch double, is pumped after scoring on Jayson Werth's single to give the Phils a 3-2 lead.

Pedro Feliz delivers the World Series-winning hit, a single in the seventh that scored Eric Bruntlett (right).

Rays' Jason Bartlett is tagged out in the seventh by Carlos Ruiz on a throw from Chase Utley, who faked to first.

Brad Lidge proves to be the ultimate closer, finishing 48-for-48 in saves with the strikeout of Eric Hinske that ended the World Series.

The Flyin' Hawaiian, Shane Victorino, lives up to his nickname while joining the celebration pile.

JERRY LODRIGUSS / Staff Photographer

YONG KIM / Staff Photographer

Key Player: Cole Hamels

As a youngster growing up in San Diego, Cole Hamels dreamed about this. He dreamed about winning the World Series, about being the MVP, about hugging teammates and spraying champagne.

The reality is much better than the dream. "It's tremendous," the 24-year-old pitcher said with a bright, ear-to-ear smile after the Phillies wrapped up the World Series championship with a 4-3 win over Tampa Bay in Game 5. "I can't describe it," he said. "It's such a phenomenal experience."

The lefthander has always been destined for greatness, right from the time the Phillies drafted him in 2002.

Hamels made five starts in the postseason and the Phillies won all of them. He beat the Rays in Game 1 of the World Series, then pitched six innings of two-run ball in the rain in the first half of Game 5. The jersey he wore that night is headed to the Hall of Fame in Cooperstown, N.Y. Maybe someday he will be, too.

— *Jim Salisbury*

EwingCole

Architects, Engineers, Interior Designers and Planners of Citizens Bank Park

Citizens Bank Park

Celebrates the

Phillies™

2008 World Championship